THE

ILLUSTRATED SELF-INSTRUCTOR

IN

PHRENOLOGY AND PHYSIOLOGY,

WITH

One Hundred Engravings,

AND

A CHART OF THE CHARACTER

AS GIVEN BY

BY O. S. AND L. N. FOWLER,

PRACTICAL PHRENOLOGISTS.

Your head is the type of your mentality.
Self-knowledge is the essense of all knowledge.

NEW YORK:
FOWLER AND WELLS, PUBLISHERS
308 BROADWAY.

Boston: No. 142 Washington St. | 1857. | Philadelphia: No. 231 Arch Street

STEREOTYPED BY

BANER & PALMER

201 William st., cor. of Frankfort, N. Y.

Conditions.	Large.	Very Large.	Full.	Average	Moderate.	Small.	Cultivate.	Restrain.
Vital Temperament,	17	17	17	17	17	17	165	
Powerful or Motive.	18	18	18	18	18	18	137	
Active or Mental. -	19	19	19	19	19	19		
Excitability of ditto,	20	20	20	20	20	20	157	175
Constitution. - -	34	34	34	34	34	34		
Organic Quality. -	47	47	47	47	47	47		
Present state, - -	47	47	47	47	47	47		
Size of head, - -	48	49	49	49	49	50		
DOMESTIC GROUP.								
1. Amativeness, - -	52	52	53	53	53	54		218
2. Parental Love, - -	55	55	56	56	56	56	220	
3. Adhesiveness, - -	57	57	58	58	58	58	226	
4. Inhabitiveness, - -	60	60	61	61	61	61	232	
5. Continuity, - -	62	62	62	62	62	62	234	
SELFISH PROPENSITIES,	63	64	64	64	64	64		
E. Vitativeness, - -	64	65	65	65	65	65	236	237
6. Combativeness, -	66	66	66	66	67	67	239	240
7. Destructiveness, -	67	68	69	69	69	69	242	243
8. Alimentiveness, -	70	70	70	71	71	71	245	246
9. Acquisitiveness, -	72	73	73	73	74	74	249	250
10. Secretiveness, - -	75	75	76	76	76	77	252	253
11. Cautiousness, - -	78	78	78	78	79	79	255	256
12. Approbativeness, -	79	80	80	80	80	81	258	259
13. Self-Esteem, - -	82	82	82	83	83	83	261	262
14. Firmness, - - -	84	85	85	85	85	85	265	266
MORAL FACULTIES,	86	86	86	86	86	86	268	270
15. Conscientiousness. -	87	88	88	88	89	89	268	270
16. Hope, - - -	89	90	90	90	90	91	272	273

Conditions.	Large.	Very Large.	Full.	Average	Moderate.	Small.	Cultivate.	Restrain.
17. Spirituality, - -	91	92	92	[illegible]	92	92	276	277
18. Veneration, - -	92	93	94	94	94	94	279	280
19. Benevolence, - -	94	95	96	96	96	96	282	283
20. Constructiveness, -	96	97	97	97	97	97	285	286
21. Ideality, - -	98	98	98	99	99	99	288	289
B. Sublimity, -	99	100	100	100	100	100	290	291
22. Imitation, - - -	100	101	101	102	102	102	293	294
23. Mirthfulness, - -	103	103	103	103	103	104	296	297
INTELLECTUAL FACULT.,	104	104	104	104	105	105		
PERCEPTIVE FACULTIES,	105	105	105	105	106	106		
24. Individuality, - -	107	107	107	107	107	108	424	
25. Form, - - -	108	108	109	109	109	109	437	
26. Size, - - - -	109	109	110	110	110	110	441	
27. Weight, - - -	110	110	110	110	110	110	446	
28. Color, - - -	111	111	111	111	111	111	450	
29. Order, - - -	112	112	112	112	112	112	456	
30. Calculation, - -	113	113	113	114	114	114	460	
31. Locality, - - -	114	114	114	114	114	115	467	
LITERARY FACULTIES,	115	115	115	115	115	115		
32. Eventuality, - -	116	116	116	117	117	117	476	
33. Time, - -	117	117	117	117	117	117	491	
34. Tune, - - -	118	118	118	118	118	118	504	506
35. Language, - -	119	119	120	120	120	120	515	
REASONING FACULTIES,	121	121	121	121	121	121		
36. Causality, - -	122	122	123	123	123	123	548	
37 Comparison, -	123	124	124	124	124	125	536	
D. Human Nature, -	125	125	125	125	125	125	540	
D. Agreeableness, -	126	126	126	126	126	126	299	273

SYMBOLICAL HEAD.

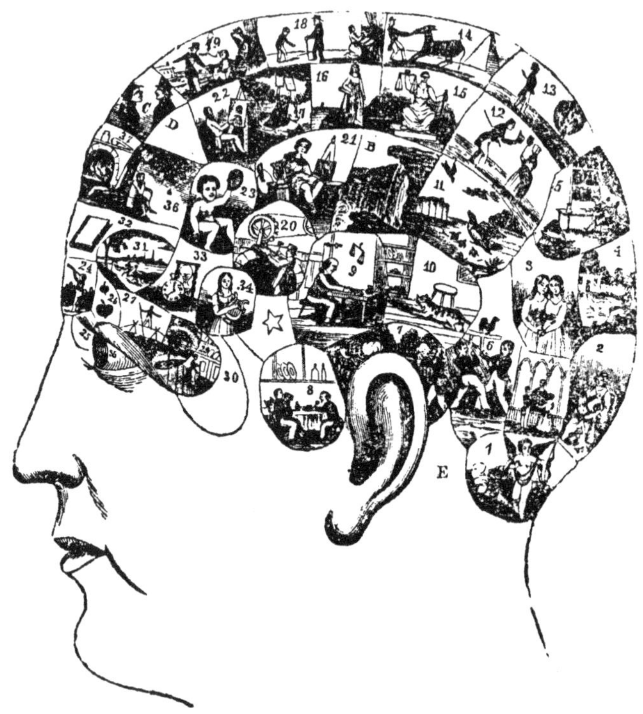

NUMBERING AND DEFINITION OF THE ORGANS.

1. AMATIVENESS, Sexual and connubial love.
2. PHILOPROGENITIVENESS, Parental love.
3. ADHESIVENESS, Friendship—sociability.
A. UNION FOR LIFE, Love of one only.
4. INHABITIVENESS, Love of home.
5. CONTINUITY, One thing at a time.
6. COMBATIVENESS, Resistance—defence.
7. DESTRUCTIVENESS, Executiveness-force.
8. ALIMENTIVENESS, Appetite, hunger.
9. ACQUISITIVENESS, Accumulation.
10. SECRETIVENESS, Policy—management.
11. CAUTIOUSNESS, Prudence, provision.
12. APPROBATIVENESS, Ambition—display.
13. SELF-ESTEEM, Self-respect—dignity.
14. FIRMNESS, Decision—perseverance.
15. CONSCIENTIOUSNESS, Justice—equity
16. HOPE, Expectation—enterprise.
17. SPIRITUALITY, Intuition--spiritual revery
18. VENERATION, Devotion—respect.
19. BENEVOLENCE, Kindness—goodness.
20. CONSTRUCTIVNESS, Mechanical ingenuity
21. IDEALITY, Refinement--taste—purity
B. SUBLIMITY, Love of grandeur.
22. IMITATION, Copying—patterning.
23. MIRTHFULNESS, Jocoseness—wit—fun.
24. INDIVIDUALITY, Observation.
25. FORM, Recollection of shape.
26. SIZE, Measuring by the eye.
27. WEIGHT, Balancing—climbing.
28. COLOR, Judgment of colors.
29. ORDER, Method—system—arrangement.
30. CALCULATION, Mental arithmetic.
31. LOCALITY. Recollection of places.
32. EVENTUALITY, Memory of facts.
33. TIME, Cognizance of duration.
34. TUNE, Music—melody by ear.
35. LANGUAGE, Expression of ideas.
36. CAUSALITY, Applying causes to effects
37. COMPARISON, inductive reasoning.
C. HUMAN NATURE, perception of motives
D. AGREEABLENESS, Pleasantness—suavity

PREFACE AND EXPLANATION.

To TEACH LEARNERS those organic conditions which indicate character, is the first object of this manual; and in order to render it accessible to all, it condenses facts and conditions, rather than elaborates arguments—because to EXPOUND Phrenology is its highest proof—states laws and results, and leaves them upon their naked merits; embodies recent discoveries; and crowds into the fewest possible words and pages just what learners need to know; and, hence, requires to be STUDIED rather than merely read. "Short, yet clear," is its motto. Its numerous illustrative engravings give the results of very extensive professional observations and experience.

To RECORD CHARACTER is its second object. In doing this, it describes those organic conditions which affect and indicate character in SEVEN degrees of power—large, very large, full, average, moderate, small, and very small, and refers those who have their physiological and phrenological conditions correctly marked in the accompanying tables, to those paragraphs which both describe themselves, and also contain specific directions how to PERFECT THEIR characters and improve children. Its plan for recording character is seen at a glance in the following

EXPLANATION OF THE TABLES.

Those physiological and phrenological conditions marked LARGE have a powerful and almost CONTROLLING influence over feelings and conduct, both single and in combination, and engross weaker ones into their service. VERY LARGE organic conditions are sovereign kings over character and conduct, and singly and in combination with each other, or with large organs, direct and sway their possessor. FULL organs play subordinate parts, yet are seen and felt, and exert more real than apparent influence. AVERAGE ones have considerable, yet a limited influence, but it is mainly in COMBINATION with large ones, though they affect character more than they seem to. MODERATE faculties are below par in fact, and still more so in appearance ; exert a limited influence; and leave character defective in these respects. SMALL organs are so deficient as easily to be perceived ; leave their possessor weak and faulty in these points ; and should be assiduously cultivated ; while VERY SMALL ones render him almost idiotic in these functions.

This table is so constructed as to record the ACTUAL POWER, or quality and quantity of the physical and mental functions, as deduced from size and activity combined, and this is done by means of dots or written figures placed opposite the names of the organs and temperaments, and the printed figures in the squares thus marked, designate the number of the page in this work which contains the corresponding description of character; and these paragraphs, thus referred to in the body of the work, have figures attached to them, referring to the pages of "Fowler's Phrenology," where an elaborate description of the several functions are discussed at length, with numerous combinations which shade and tone the character.

The six left hand columns refer to the pages of this work, while the two right hand ones refer to those NUMBERED PARAGRAPHS found throughout "Physiology," "Self-Culture," and "Memory," which contain directions for cultivating, restraining, and rightly directing whatever physical functions or mental faculties may require either, both in adults and children; so that these works, in conjunction with a correct marking in these tables, furnish a complete directory for obviating faults, supplying defects, developing excellencies, and perfecting one's self and children.

Faculties marked with an upward curve, thus, ⌒, in the several squares, are deficient, and require cultivation; while those marked with a downward curve, thus, ⌣, are liable to excess or perversion, and should be carefully guarded and rightly directed; while + signifies about one third larger; and — one third smaller than a dot would indicate in the same place, thus rendering the scale equal to twenty-one.

MARKING THE CHART BY FIGURES.

Some persons who record examinations prefer to use numerals to indicate the size of the organs. We describe the organs in seven degrees of power, and to indicate those degrees, employ the written figures, 1, 2, 3, 4, 5, 6, 7. When thus used, 1 means VERY SMALL; 2, SMALL; 3 MODERATE; 4, AVERAGE; 5, FULL; 6, LARGE; 7, VERY LARGE. The signs + —, ⌒, ⌣, mean the same as in the above table.

THE SELF-INSTRUCTOR.

SECTION I.

PHYSIOLOGICAL CONDITIONS AS AFFECTING AND INDICATING CHARACTER.

I.—VALUE OF SELF-KNOWLEDGE.

"KNOWLEDGE is power"—to accomplish, to enjoy—and these are the only ends for which man was created. ALL knowledge confers this power. Thus, how incalculably, and in how many ways, have recent discoveries in chemistry enhanced human happiness, of which the lucifer match furnishes a *home* example. Increasing knowledge in agriculture is doubling the means of human sustenance. How immeasurably have modern mechanical improvements multiplied, and cheapened all the comforts of life. How greatly have steamboats and railroads added to the former stock of human success and pleasures. Similar remarks apply to all other kinds of knowledge, and as it increases from age to age will it proportionally multiply all forms of human happiness. In fact, its inherent *nature* and legitimate effect is to promote every species of enjoyment and success. Other things being equal, those who know most, by a law of things, can both accomplish and enjoy most; while ignorance instead of being bliss, is the greatest cause of human weakness, wickedness, and woe. Hence, to ENLIGHTEN man, is *the* way to reform and perfect him.

But SELF-knowledge is, of all its other kinds, both the most useful and promotive of personal and universal happiness and success. "Know thyself" was written, in golden capitals, upon the splendid temple of Delphos, as the most important maxim the wise men of Greece could transmit to unborn generations; and the Scriptures wisely command us to "search our own hearts." Since all happiness flows from obeying, and all pain from violating, the LAWS OF OUR BEING, to know our own selves is to know these laws, and becomes the first step in the road of their obedience, which is life. Self-knowledge, by teaching the laws and conditions of life and health, becomes the most efficacious means of prolonging the former and increasing the latter—both of which are *paramount* conditions of enjoying and accomplishing. It also shows us our natural talents, capabilities, virtues, vices, strong and weak points, liabilities to err, etc., and thereby points out, unmistakably, those occupations and spheres in which we can and cannot succeed and shine; and develops the laws and conditions of human and personal virtue and moral perfection, as well as of vice, and how to avoid it. It is, therefore, the quintessence of all knowledge; places its possessor upon the very acme of enjoyment and perfection; and bestows the highest powers and richest treasures mortals can possess. In short, to know ourselves perfectly, is to know every law of our being, every condition cf happiness, and every cause of suffering; and to *practice* such knowledge, is to render ourselves as perfectly happy, throughout every department of our being, as we can possibly be and live. And since nothing in nature stands alone, but each is reciprocally related to all, and all, collectively, form one magnificent whole—since all stars and worlds mutually act and react upon each other, to cause day and night, summer and winter, sun and rain, blossom and fruit; since every genus, species, and individual throughout nature is second or sixteenth cousin to every other; and since man is the epitome of universal nature, the embodiment of all her functions, the focus of all her light, and representative of all her perfections—of course to understand *him* thoroughly is to know *all* things. Nor can nature be studied advantageously without him for a text-book, nor he without her.

Moreover, since man is composed of mind *and* body, both reciprocally and most intimately related to each other—since his mentality is manifested only by bodily organs, and the latter depends wholly upon the former, of course his mind can be studied only through its ORGANIC relations. If it were manifested independently of his physiology, it might be studied separately, but since all his organic conditions modify his mentality, the two must be studied TOGETHER. Heretofore humanity has been studied by piece-meal. Anatomists have investigated only his organic structure, and there stopped; and mental philosophers have studied him metaphysically, wholly regardless of all his physiological relations; while theologians have theorized upon his moral faculties alone; and hence their utter barrenness, from Aristotle down. As if one should study nothing but the trunk of a tree, another only its roots, a third its leaves, or fruit, without compounding their researches, of what value is such piece-meal study? If the physical man constituted one whole being, and the mental another, their separate study might be useful; but since all we know of mind, and can do with it, is manifested and done wholly by means of physical instruments—especially since every possible condition and change of the physiology correspondingly affects the mentality—of course their MUTUAL relations, and the laws of their RECIPROCAL action, must be investigated *collectively*. Besides, every mental philosopher has deduced his system from his own closet cogitations, and hence their babel-like confusion. But within the last half century, a new star, or rather sun, has arisen upon the horizon of mind—a sun which puts the finger of SCIENTIFIC CERTAINTY upon every mental faculty, and discloses those *physiological* conditions which affect, increase or diminish, purify or corrupt, or in any other way modify, either the mind itself, or its products—thought, feeling, and character—and thereby reduces mental study to that same *tangible* basis of *proportion* in which all science consists; leaving nothing dark or doubtful, but developing the true SCIENCE OF MIND, and the laws of its action. Of this, the greatest of all discoveries, Gall was the author, and Phrenology and Physiology the instruments which conjointly embrace whatever appertains to mind, and to man, in all his organic relations, show how to perfect the former by improving the latter, and disclose specific SIGNS OF CHARACTER, by which we may know ourselves and our fellow-men with certainty—a species of knowledge most delightful in acquisition, and valuable in application.

2.—STRUCTURE CORRESPONDS WITH CHARACTER.

Throughout universal nature, the structure of all things is powerful or weak, hard or soft, coarse or fine, etc., in accordance with its functions; and in this there is a philosophical fitness or adaptation. What immense power of function trees put forth, to rear and sustain aloft, at such great mechanical disadvantage, their ponderous load and vast canvas of leaves, limbs, and fruit or seeds, spread out to all the surgings of tempestuous winds and storms; and the *texture* of wood is as compact and firm as its functional power is prodigious. Hence its value as timber. But tender vegetables, grains, etc., require little power, and accordingly are fragile in structure. Lions, tigers, hyenas, and all powerfully strong beasts, have a correspondingly powerful organic structure. The muscular strength of lions is so extraordinary, that seizing wild cattle by the neck, they dash through thicket, marsh, and ravine, for hours together, as a cat would drag a squirrel, and their roar is most terrific; and so powerful is their structure, that it took Drs. McClintock, Allen, myself, and two experienced "resurrectionists," FOUR HOURS, though we worked with might and main, just to cut off a magnificent Numidian lion's head. So hard and tough were the muscles and tendons of his neck, that cutting them seemed like severing wire, and after slitting all we could, we were finally obliged to employ a powerful purchase to start them. It took over three hard days' work to remove his skin. So compact are the skins of the elephant, rhinoceros, alligator, and some other animals of great muscular might, that rifle-balls, shot against them, flatten and fall at their feet—their structure being as dense as their strength is mighty—while feeble animals have a correspondingly soft structure. In like manner, the flesh of strong persons is dense and most elastic, while those of weakly ones are flabby, and yield to pressure.

Moreover, fineness of texture manifests exquisiteness of sensibility, as seen by contrasting human organism and feelings with brutes, or fine-haired persons with coarse-haired. Of course, a similar relation and adaptation exist between all other organic characteristics and their functions. In short, it is a LAW as philosophical as universal, that the structure of all beings, and of each of their organs, corresponds perfectly with their functions—a law based in the very nature and fitness of things, and governing all shades and diversities of organization and manifestation. Accordingly those who are coarse-skinned are coarse in feeling, and coarse-grained throughout; while those finely organized are fine-minded, and thus of all other textures of hair, skin, etc.

3.—SHAPE CORRESPONDS WITH CHARACTER.

Matter, in its primeval state, was "without form, and void," or gaseous, but slowly condensing, it solidified or CRYSTALLIZED into minerals and rocks—and all rocks and minerals are crystalline—which, decomposed by sun and air, form soil, and finally assume organic, or animal and vegetable forms. All crystals assume *angular* forms, and all vegetables and animals those more or less *spherical*, as seeds, fruits, etc., in proportion as they are lower or higher in the creative scale; though other conditions sometimes modify this result.

Nature also manifests certain types of character in and by corresponding types of form. Thus all trees bear a general resemblance to all other trees in growth and general character, and also in shape; and those most nearly allied in character approximate in shape, as pine, hemlock, firs, etc., while every tree of a given kind is shaped like all others of that kind, in bark, limb, leaf, and fruit. So all grains, grasses, fruits, and every bear, horse, elephant, and human being bear a close resemblance to all others of its kind, both in character and configuration, and on this resemblance all scientific classification is based. And, since this general correspondence exists between all the divisions and subdivisions into classes, genera, and species of nature's works, of course the resemblance is perfect between *all the details* of outward forms and inward mental characteristics; for this law, seen to govern nature in the outline, must of course govern her in all her minutest details; so that every existing outward shape is but the mirrored reflection of its inner likeness. Moreover, since nature always clothes like mentalities in like shapes, as oak, pine, apple, and other trees, and all lions, sheep, fish, etc., in other general types of form, of course the more nearly any two beings approximate to each other in mental disposition, do they resemble each other in shape. Thus, not only do tiger form and character always accompany each other, but leopards, panthers, cats, and all feline species resemble this tiger shape more or less closely, according as their dispositions approach or depart from his; and monkeys approach nearer to the human shape, and also mentality, than any other animal except orang-outangs, which are still more human both in shape and character, and form the connecting link between man and brute. How absolute and universal, therefore, the correspondence, both in general outline and minute detail, between shape and character. Hence the shape of all things becomes a sure index of its mentality.

4.—RESEMBLANCE BETWEEN HUMAN AND ANIMAL PHYSIOGNOMY AND CHARACTER.

Moreover, some men closely resemble one or another of the animal species, in both looks and character; that is, have the eagle, or bull-dog, or lion or baboon expression of face, and when they do, have the corres-

THE LION FACE.

DANIEL WEBSTER.

ponding characteristics. Thus the lion's head and face are broad and stout built, with a heavy beard and mane, and a mouth rendered square by small front and large eye teeth, and its corners slightly turning downward; and that human " Lion of the North"—who takes hold only of some great undertaking, which he pursues with indomitable energy, rarely pounces on his prey, but when he does, so roars that a nation quakes; demolishes his victim; and is an intellectual king among men—bears no slight physiognomical resemblance in his stout form, square face and mouth, large nose, and open countenance, to the king of beasts.

TRISTAM BURGESS, called in Congress the "Bald Eagle,' from his having the aquiline or eagle-bill nose, a projection in the upper lip, falling into an indentation in the lower, his eagle-shaped eyes and eyebrows, as seen in the accompanying engraving, eagle-like in character, was the

THE EAGLE FACE.

No. 2. TRISTAM BURGESS.

most sarcastic, tearing, and soaring man of his day, John Randolph excepted. And whoever has a long, hooked, hawk-bill, or common nose, wide mouth, spare form, prominence at the lower and middle part of the forehead, is very fierce when assailed, high tempered, vindictive, efficient, and aspiring, and will fly higher and farther than others.

TIGERS are always spare, muscular, long, full over the eyes, large-mouthed, and have eyes slanting downward from their outer to inner angles; and human beings thus physiognomically characterized, are fierce, domineering, revengeful, most enterprising, not over humane, a terror to enemies, and conspicuous somewhere.

BULL-DOGS, generally fleshy, square-mouthed—because their tusks project and front teeth retire—broad-headed, indolent unless roused, but then terribly fierce, have their correspondent men and women, whose growling, coarse, heavy voices, full habit, logy yet powerful motions, square face, down-turned corners of mouth, and general physiognomical cast betoken their second-cousin relationship to this growling, biting race, of which the old line-tender at the Newburgh dock is a sample.

SWINE—fat, logy, lazy, good-dispositioned, flat and hollow-nosed—have their cousins in large-abdomened, pud-nosed, double-chinned, talkative, story-enjoying, beer-loving, good-feeling, yes, yes, humans, who love some easy business, and hate HARD work.

Horses, oxen, sheep, owls, doves, snakes, and even frogs, etc., also have their men and women cousins, together with their accompanying characters.

These resemblances are more difficult to describe than to recognize; but the forms of mouth, nose, and chin, and sound of voice, are the best basis of observation.

5.—BEAUTIFUL, HOMELY, AND OTHER FORMS.

In accordance with this general law, that shape is as character, well-proportioned persons have harmony of features, and well-balanced minds; whereas those, some of whose features stick right out, and others fall far in, have uneven, ill-balanced characters, so that homely, disjointed exteriors indicate corresponding interiors, while evenly-balanced and exquisitely formed men and women have well-balanced and susceptible mentalities. Hence, women, more beautiful than men, have finer feelings, and greater perfection of character, yet are less powerful—and the more beautifully formed the woman the more exquisite and perfect her mentality. True, some handsome women often make the greatest scolds, just as the sweetest things, when soured, become correspondingly sour. The finest things, when perverted, become the worst. These two extremes are the worst tempered—those naturally beautiful and fine skinned, become so exquisitely organized, that when perverted they are proportionally bad, and those naturally ugly-formed, become ugly by nature.

Yet ordinary-looking persons are often excellent dispositioned, benevolent, talented, etc., because they have a few POWERFUL traits, and also features—the very thing we are explaining; that is, they have EXTREMES alike of face and character. Thus it is that every diversity of character has its correspondence in both the organic texture and physiognomical form. To elucidate this subject fully we must explain another law, that of

6.—HOMOGENEOUSNESS, OR ONENESS OF STRUCTURE.

Every part of every thing bears an exact correspondence to that thing AS A WHOLE. Thus, tall-bodied trees have long branches and leaves, and short-bodied trees, short branches and roots; while creeping vines, as the grape, honey-suckle, etc., have long, slim roots that run under ground as extensively as their tops do above. The Rhode Island greening is a large, well-proportioned apple and its tree is large in trunk, limb, leaf, and root, and symmetrical, while the gillifleur is conical and its tree long limbed and even high to a peak at the top, while flat and broad-topped trees bear wide, flat, sunken-eyed apples. Very thrifty growing trees, as the Baldwin, fall pippin, Bartlet, black Tartarian, etc., generally bear large fruit, while small fruit, as the seckle pear, lady apple, bell de choisa cherry, grow slowly, and have many small twigs and branches. Beautiful trees that bear red fruit, as the Baldwin, etc., have red inner bark; while yellow and green-colored fruits grow on trees the inner rind of whose limbs is yellow or green. Peach-trees, that bear early peaches, have deeply-notched leaves, and the converse of late ones; so that, by these and other physiognomical signs, experienced nurserymen can tell what a given tree is at first sight.

In accordance with this law of unity of structure, long-handed persons have long fingers, toes, arms, legs, bodies, heads, and phrenological organs; while short and broad-shouldered persons are short and broad-handed and fingered, faced, nosed, and limbed, and wide and low bodied. When the bones on the hand are prominent, all the bones, nose included, are generally so, and thus of all other characteristics of the hand and any other part of the body. Hence, let a hand be thrust through a hole, and I will tell the general character of its owner, because if it is large or small, hard or soft, strong or weak, firm or flabby, coarse-grained or fine-textured, even or prominent, rough or smooth, small-boned or large-boned, or whatever else, his whole body is built upon the same principle, with which his brain and mentality also correspond. Hence small-nosed persons have little soul, and large-nosed a great deal of character of some kind; large nostrils indicate powerful lungs and bodies; while narrow nostrils indicate weak ones. Flat noses indicate flat minds, and prominent noses strong points of character; sharp noses, keen, clear intellects and intense feelings; blunt noses, obtuse minds; long noses, long heads; hollow noses, tame characters; finely-formed noses, well-proportioned character, etc.; and thus of every part of the body. And it is meet philosophical, accordant with the principles of adaptation, that this should be thus; and renders observations on character easy and correct In general, too, tall persons have high heads, and are more aspiring, aim high, and seek conspicuosity, while short ones have flat heads, and seek worldly pleasures. Tall persons are rarely mean, though often grasping; but very penurious persons are often broad built. Small persons generally have exquisite mentalities, yet less power; while great men are rarely dwarfs, though great size often co-exists with sluggishness. To particularize—there are four leading forms which indicate generic characteristics, all existing in every one, yet in different DEGREES. They are these:

7.—THE BROAD, OR VITAL STRUCTURE.

Thus, Indian ponies are broad built or thick set, and accordingly very tough, hardy, enduring of labor, and tenacious of life, yet less active and nimble Bull-dogs, elephants, and all round-favored animals and men,

THE VITAL, OR ANIMAL TEMPERAMENT.

No. 3. HALL.

also illustrate this law. Rotundity, with a moderate-sized head, indicates ancestral longevity; and, unless health has been abused, renders it possessor strong constitutioned, slow to ripen, or better as they grow older; full of animal life; self-caring; money-making; fond of animal pleasures; good feeling, yet spirited when roused; impulsive; more given to physical than mental action; better adapted to business than study, and talking than writing; more eloquent than argumentative; wide rather than high or long headed; more glowing than cool in feeling; and more enthusiastic than logical or deep. The preceding likeness represents this class, and his ancestors exceeded 100. He has never been sick; can endure any thing, and can never sit much in doors.

8.—THE MUSCULAR, OR POWERFUL TEMPERAMENT,

Gives projecting features, bones, noses, eyebrows, etc., with distinctness of muscle; and renders its possessors strong; tough; thorough going; forcible; easy, yet powerful of motion; perhaps slow, but very stout; strongly marked, if not idiosyncratic; determined; and impressive.

PROMINENT, OR POWERFUL.

No. 4. ALEXANDER CAMPBELL.

both physically and mentally, who stamp their character on all they touch, of whom Alexander Campbell is a good example.

9.—THE LONG, OR ACTIVE FORM,

Gives ACTIVITY. Thus the gazelle, deer greyhound, weasel, and all long and slim animals, are sprightly, light-motioned, agile, quick, nimble, and full of action; and those persons thus formed are restless, wide awake, always doing, eager, uncommonly quick to think and feel, sprightly in conversation, versatile in talent, flexible, suggestive, abounding in idea, apt at most things; exposed to consumption, because their action exceeds their strength, early ripe, brilliant, and liable to premature exhaustion and disease, because the mentality predominates over the vitality; of which Captain Knight, of the ship "New World," who has a world-wide reputation for activity, enterprise, daring, impetuousness, promptness, judgment, earnestness of execution, affability, and sprightliness, furnishes a good example.

LONG, OR ACTIVE.

No. 5. CAPT. KNIGHT.

10.—THE SHARP AND ANGULAR, OR MENTAL ORGANIZATION,

Have ardent desires; intense feelings; keen susceptibilities; enjoy and suffer in the extreme; are whole-souled; sensitive; positive in likes and dislikes; cordial; enthusiastic; impulsive; have their hobbies; abound in good feeling, yet are quick-tempered; excitable; liable to extremes; too much creatures of feeling, and have a great deal of what we call SOUL, or passion, or warmth of feeling. This temperament prevails in BRILLIANT writers or speakers, who are too refined and sensitive for the mass of mankind. They gleam in their career of genius, and are liable to burn out their vital powers on the altar of nervous excitability, and like Pollok, H. K. White, McDonald Clarke, or Leggett, fall victims to premature death. Early attention to the physical training of children, would spare to the world the lives and usefulness of some of the brightest stars in the firmament of science

No. 6. Voltaire.

11.—COMBINATIONS OF TEMPERAMENT.

These shapes, or structures, called temperaments, however, never exist separately; yet since all may be strong, or all weak, or either predominant or deficient, of course their COMBINATIONS with each other and with the Phrenology exert potent influences over character, and put the observer in possession of both the outline and the inner temple of character.

Breadth of organization gives endurance, animal power, and animal feelings; and sharpness gives intensity of action, along with mind as mind and the two united, give both that rapidity and clearness of mind and that intense glow of feeling which make the orator. Accordingly, all truly eloquent men will be found to be broad built, round-shouldered, portly, and fleshy, and yet rather sharp-featured. Of these, Sidney Smith furnishes a sample.

His nose indicates the sharpness of the mental temperament, and his fullness of face the breadth of the animal—the blending of which gives

THE EXCITABLE, ORATORICAL, OR MENTAL VITAL.

No. 7. Sidney Smith.

that condensation of fervor and intellectuality which make him Sidney Smith. Intensity of feeling is the leading element of good speaking, for this excites feeling, and moves the masses. Wirt had this temperament. It predominates in Preston, and in every man noted for eloquence.

The sharp and broad, combined with smallness of stature, is still more susceptible, yet lacks strength. Such will be extremely happy, or most miserable, or both, and are liable to die young, because their action is too great for their endurance.

The vital mental, or broad and sharp, gives great power of constitution. excellent lungs and stomach, strong enjoying susceptibilities intense love of pleasure, a happy, ease-loving cast of body and mind; powerful passions, most intense feelings, and a story and song-loving disposition, and, with large Tune, superior singing powers. This is, PAR EXCELLENCE, the singing temperament. It also loves poetry and eloquence, and often executes them. Of this organism, its accompanying character, Dempster, furnishes an excellent example.

ND SHARP ORGANIZATION.

No. 8. Dempster.

VITAL MOTIVE.

No. 9. Phineas Stevens.

The Vital Motive Apparatus, or powerful and animal temperament, is indicated by the broad and prominent in shape, and renders its possessor of good size and height, if not large; well-proportioned; broad-shouldered; muscular, nose and cheek-bones prominent; visage strongly marked; features often coarse and homely; countenance stern and harsh; face red; hair red or sandy, if not coarse; and movements strong, but often awkward, and seldom polished. He will be best adapted to some laborious occupation, and enjoy hard work more than books or literary pursuits; have great power of feeling, and thus require much self government; possess more talent than he exhibits to others, manifest his mind more in his business, in creating resources and managing matters, than in literary pursuits or mind as such; and improve with age, growing better and more intellectual as he grows older; and manufactures as much animal steam as he can work off, even if he works all the time hard. Such men ACCOMPLISH; are strong-minded; sensible; hard to beat; indomitable; often impulsive; and strong in passion when once aroused; as well as often excellent men. Yet this temperament is capable of being depraved, especially if the subject drinks. Sailors usually have this temperament, because fresh air and hard work induce it.

PROMINENT AND SHARP

No. 10. Dr. Caldwell.

The Motive Mental Temperament, or the prominent and sharp in structure, with the motive predominant, and the vital average or full, is of good size; rather tall and slim; lean and raw-boned, if not homely and awkward; poor in flesh; bones and features prominent, particularly the nose; a firm and distinct muscle, and a good physical organization; a keen, piercing, penetrating eye; the front upper teeth rather large and projecting; the hands, fingers, and limbs all long; a long face, and often a high forehead; a firm, rapid, energetic walk; and great ease and efficiency of action, accompanied with little fatigue.

He will have strong desires, and much energy of character; will take hold of projects with both hands, and drive forward in spite of obstacles, and hence is calculated to accomplish a great deal; is not idle or lazy, but generally prefers to wait upon himself; will move, walk, etc. in a decided, forcible, and straightforward manner; have strong passions; a tough and wiry brain and body; a strong and vigorous mind; good judgment; a clear head, and talents more solid than brilliant; be long-headed; bold; cool; calculating; fond of deep reasoning and philosophizing, of hard thinking, and the graver and more solid branches of learning. This is the thorough-going temperament; imparts business powers; predisposes to hard work, and is indispensable to those who engage in great undertakings, or who would rise to eminence.

One having the mental temperament predominant, the motive full or large, and the vital average to full, will differ in build from the preceding description only in his being smaller, taller in proportion, and more spare. He will have a reflective, thinking, planning, discriminating cast of mind; a great fondness for literature, science, and intellectual pursuits of the deeper, graver kind; be inclined to choose a professional or mental occupation; to exercise his body much, but his mind more; will have a high forehead; good moral faculties; and the brain developed more from the root of the nose, over to Philoprogenitiveness, than around the ears. In character, also, the moral and intellectual faculties will predominate. This temperament is seldom connected with depravity, but generally with talent, and a manifestation, not only of superior talents, but of the solid, metaphysical, reasoning, investigating intellect; a fondness for natural philosophy the natural sciences, etc. It is also the temperament for authorship and clear-headed, labored productions. It predominates in Revs. Jonathan Edwards, Wilbur Fiske, N. Taylor, E. A. Parke, Leonard Bacon, Albert Barnes, Oberlin, and Pres. Day; Drs. Parish and Rush: in Hitchcock, Jas. Brown, the grammarian, ex-U. S. Attorney-General Butler, Hugh L. White, Wise, Asher Robbins, Walter Jones, Esq., of Washington, D. C.,

THE MENTAL MOTIVE TEMPERAMENT.

No. 11. William Cullen Bryant.

Franklin, Alex. Hamilton, Chief-Justice Marshall, Calhoun, John Q. Adams, Percival, Noah Webster, Geo. Combe, Lucretia Mott, Catharine Waterman, Mrs. Sigourney, and nearly every distinguished author and scholar. The accompanying engraving of William Cullen Bryant furnishes as excellent an illustration of the shape that accompanies this temperament, as his character does of its accompanying mentality.

The Long and Sharp combine the highest order of action and energy with promptness, clearness, and untiring assiduity, and considerable power. Such are best fitted for some light, active business, requiring more brightness and quickness than power, such as merchants.

THE ORGANS THAT ACCOMPANY GIVEN TEMPERAMENTS.—Not only do certain outlines of character and drifts of talent go along with certain kinds of organizations, but certain phrenological developments accompany certain temperaments. As the pepper secretes the smarting, the sugar-cane sweetness, castor-beans and whales, oil, etc., throughout nature, so certain temperaments secrete more brain than others; and some, brain in particular regions of the head; and others, brain in other regions of the head—but all form most of those organs best adapted to carry out those characteristics already shown to accompany the several temperaments. Thus, the vital or animal temperament secretes brain in the neighborhood of the ears, so that along with breadth of body goes that width of head which gives that full development of the animal organs which is required by the animal temperament. Thus, breadth of form, width of head, and animality of temperament and character, all go together.

PROMINENCE of organization, or the motive or powerful temperament, gives force of character, and secretes brain in the crown of the head, and over the eyes, along with Combativeness, Destructiveness, Appetite, and Acquisitiveness. These are the very organs required by this temperament; for they complete that force which embodies the leading element of this organization. I never saw this temperament unaccompanied with prodigious Firmness, and great Combativeness and perceptives.

MENTAL VITAL.

No. 12. FANNY FORRESTER.

THE MENTAL VITAL.—The finest and most exquisite organization is that which unites the mental in predominance with the animal, the prominent retiring. In this case, the person is rather short, the form light, the face and person full, and the hair brown or auburn, or between the two. It will sometimes be found in men, but much oftener in women. It is the feeling, sentimental, exalted, angelic temperament; and always imparts purity, sweetness, devotion, exquisiteness, susceptibility, loveliness, and great moral worth.

The phrenological organs which accompany this temperament, are smaller Firmness, deficient Self-Esteem, large or very large Approbative ness, smaller Destructiveness, Appetite not large, Adhesiveness and Philoprogenitiveness very large, Amativeness fair; the head wide, not directly round the ears, but at the upper part of the sides, including Ideality, Mirthfulness, Sublimity, and Cautiousness; and a fine top head, rising at Benevolence quite as much as at Firmness, and being wide on the top, whereas the motive temperament gives perhaps a ridge in the middle of the head, but not breadth on the top, and leaves the head much higher at the back part than at Benevolence. Benevolence, however, often accompanies the animal temperament, and especially that quiet goodness which grants favors because the donor is too pliable, or too easy, to refuse them. But for tenderness of sympathy, and whole-souled interest for mankind, no temperament is equal to the vital mental. The motive mental, however, is the one most common in reformers. The reason is this. The mentality imparted by this temperament sees the miseries of mankind, and weeps over them; and the force of character imparted by it pushes vigorously plans for their amelioration. The outer portion of Causality, which plans, often accompanies the animal temperament; the inner, which reasons, the motive mental and mental.

A WELL-BALANCED ORGANIZATION.

No. 13. WASHINGTON.

The more perfect these organic conditions, the better. Greater breadth than sharpness, or more vitality than action, causes sluggishness, dullness of feeling, and inertness, while too great action for strength, wears out its possessor prematurely. More prominence than sharpness, leaves talents latent, or undeveloped, while predominant sharpness and breadth, give such exquisite sensibilities, as that many things harrow up all the finer sensibilities of keen-feeling souls. But when all are powerful and EQUALLY BALANCED, they combine all the conditions of power, activity, and susceptibility; allow neither icy coldness, nor passion's burning heat, but unite cool judgment, intense but well-governed feelings, great force of both character and intellect, and perfect consistency and discretion.

with extraordinary energy ; sound common sense, and far-seeing sagacity, with brilliancy ; and bestow the highest order of Physiology and Phrenology. Such an organization and character were those of WASHINGTON.

Besides these prominent signs of character, there are many others, among which,

12.—THE LAUGH CORRESPONDS WITH THE CHARACTER.

Those who laugh very heartily, have much cordiality and whole-souledness of character, except that those who laugh heartily at trifles, have much feeling, yet little sense. Those whose giggles are rapid, but light, have much intensity of feeling, yet lack power; whereas those who combine rapidity with force in laughing, combine them in character. One of the greatest workers I ever employed, I hired just because he laughed heartily, and he worked just as he laughed. But a colored domestic who laughed very rapidly, but LIGHTLY, took a great many steps to do almost nothing, and though she worked fast, accomplished little. Vulgar persons always laugh vulgarly, and refined persons show refinement in their laugh. Those who ha, ha, right out, unreservedly, have no cunning, and are open-hearted in every thing; while those who suppress laughter, and try to control their countenances in it, are more or less secretive. Those who laugh with their mouth closed, are non-committal; while those who throw it wide open, are unguarded and unequivocal in character. Those who, suppressing laughter for a while, burst forth volcano-like, have strong characteristics, but are well governed, yet violent when they give way to their feelings. Then there is the intellectual laugh, the love laugh, the horse laugh, the Philoprogenitive laugh, the friendly laugh, and many other kinds of laugh, each indicative of corresponding mental developments.

13.—THE WALK AS INDICATING CHARACTER.

As already shown, texture corresponds to character, and motion to texture, and therefore to character. Those whose motions are awkward, yet easy, possess much efficiency and positiveness of character, yet lack polish; and just in proportion as they become refined in mind, will their mode of carriage be correspondingly improved. A short and quick step, indicates a brisk and active, but rather contracted mind, whereas those who take long steps, generally have long heads; yet if their step be slow, they will make comparatively little progress, while those whose step is LONG AND QUICK, will accomplish proportionately much, and pass most of their competitors on the highway of life. Their heads and plans, too, will partake of the same far-reaching character evinced in their carriage. Those who sluff or drag their heels, drag and drawl in every thing; while those who walk with a springing, bounding step, abound in mental snap and spring. Those whose walk is mincing, affected, and artificial, rarely, if ever, accomplish much; whereas those who walk carelessly, that is, naturally, are just what they appear to be, and put on nothing for outside show. Those who, in walking, roll from side to side, lack directness of character, and side every way, according to circumstances; whereas, those who take a bee line—that is, whose body moves neither to the right nor left, but straight forward—have a corresponding directness of purpose, and oneness of character. (Those also who tetter up and down when they walk, rising an inch or two every step, will have many corresponding ups and downs in life, because of their irregularity of character and feeling.) Those, too, who make a great ado in walking, will make much needless parade in every thing else, and hence spend a great amount of useless steam in all they undertake, yet accomplish little; whereas those who walk easily, or expend little strength in walking, will accomplish great results with a little strength, both mentally and physically. In short, every individual has his own peculiar mode of moving, which exactly accords with his mental character; so that, as far as you can see such modes, you can decipher such outlines of character.

To DANCING, these principles apply equally. Dr. Wieting, the celebrated lecturer on physiology, once asked where he could find something on the temperaments, and was answered, "Nowhere; but if I can ever see you among men, I will give you a PRACTICAL lesson upon it." Accordingly, afterward, chance threw us together in a hotel, in which was a dancing-school that evening. Insisting on the fulfillment of our promise, we accompanied him into the dancing saloon, and pointed out, first, a small, delicately moulded, fine skinned, pocket-Venus, whose motions were light, easy, waving, and rather characterless, who put forth but little strength in dancing. We remarked—"She is very exquisite in feelings, but rather light in the upper story, lacking sense, thought, and strength of mind." Of a large, raw-boned, bouncing Betty, who threw herself far up, and came down good and solid, when she danced, we remarked—"She is one of your strong, powerful, determined characters, well suited to do up rough work, but utterly destitute of polish, though possessed of great force." Others came in for their share of criticism—some being all dandy, others all business, yet none all intellect.

14.—THE MODE OF SHAKING HANDS

Also expresses character. Thus those who give a tame and loose hand, and shake lightly, have a cold, if not heartless and selfish disposition, rarely sacrificing much for others—probably conservatives, and lack warmth of soul. But those who grasp firmly, and shake heartily, have a corresponding whole-souledness of character, are hospitable, and will sacrifice business to friends; while those who bow low when they shake cands, add deference to friendship, and are easily led, for good or bad, by friends.

15. THE MOUTH AND EYES PECULIARLY EXPRESSIVE OF CHARACTER.

Every mouth differs from every other, and indicates a coincident character. Large mouths express a corresponding quantity of mentality, while small ones indicate a lesser amount of mentality. A coarsely formed mouth indicates power of character, while one finely formed indicates exquisite susceptibilities. Hence small, delicately-formed mouths, indicate only common minds, but very fine feelings, with much perfection of character. Whenever the muscles about the mouth are distinct, the character is correspondingly positive, and the reverse. Those who open their mouths wide and frequently, thereby evince an open soul, while closed mouths, unless to hide deformed teeth, are proportionately secretive.

And thus of the eyes. In travelling west, in 1842, we examined a man who made great pretension to religion, but was destitute of Conscience, whom we afterward ascertained to be an impostor. While attending the Farmers' Club, in New York, this scamp came in, and besides keeping his eyes half closed half the time, frequently shut them so as to peep out upon those present, but opened them barely enough to secure vision. Those who keep their eyes half shut, are peekaboos and eavesdroppers, and those who use squinting glasses are no better, unless they merely copy a foolish fashion. The use of quizzing glasses indicates either defective sight or defective mentalities, but are rarely if ever employed except as a fashionable appendage.

Those, too, who keep their coats buttoned up, fancy high-necked and closed dresses, etc., are equally non-communicative, but those who like open, free, flowing garments, are equally open-hearted and communicative.

16.—INTONATIONS AS EXPRESSIVE OF CHARACTER.

Whatever makes a noise, from the deafening roar of sea, cataract, and whirlwind's mighty crash, through all forms of animal life, to the sweet and gentle voice of woman, makes a sound which agrees perfectly with its character. Thus the terrific roar of the lion, and the soft cooing of the dove, correspond exactly with their respective dispositions; while the rough and powerful bellow of the bull, the fierce yell of the tiger, the hoarse guttural moan of the hyena, and the swinish grunt, the sweet warblings of birds, in contrast with the raven's croak, and owl's hoot, each corresponds perfectly with their respective characteristics. And this law holds equally true of man—that the human intonations are as superior to brutal as human character exceeds animal. Accordingly, the peculiarities of every human being are expressed in his voice, and mode of speaking. Coarse-grained and powerfully animal organizations have a coarse harsh, and grating voice, while in exact proportion as persons become refined, and elevated mentally, will their tones of voice become correspondingly refined and perfected. We little realize how much of character we infer from this source. Thus, some female friends are visiting me transiently. A male friend, staying with me, enters the room, is seen by my female company, and his walks, dress, manners, etc., closely scrutinized, yet says nothing, and retires, leaving a comparatively indistinct impression as to his character upon my female visitors, whereas, if he simply said yes or no, the mere SOUND of his voice communicates to their minds most of his character, and serves to fix distinctly upon their minds clear and correct general ideas of his mentality.

The barbarous races use the guttural sounds, more than the civilized. Thus Indians talk more down the throat than white men, and thus of those men who are lower or higher in the human scale. Those whose voices are clear and distinct have clear minds, while those who only half form their words, or are heard indistinctly, say by deaf persons, are mentally obtuse. Those who have sharp, shrill intonations have correspondingly intense feelings, and equal sharpness both of anger and kindness, as is exemplified by every scold in the world; whereas those with smooth, or sweet voices have corresponding evenness and goodness of character. Yet contradictory as it may seem, these same persons not unfrequently combine both sharpness and softness of voice, and such always combine them in character. There is also the intellectual, the moral, the animal, the selfish, the benignant, the mirthful, the devout, the love, and many other intonations, each accompanying corresponding peculiarities of characters. In short, every individual is compelled, by every word he utters, to manifest something of his true character—a sign of character as diversified as it is correct.

17.—HAIR, SKIN, ETC., AS INDICATING CHARACTER.

Coarseness of texture indicates a coarseness of function; while a fine organization indicates a corresponding fineness of mentality. And since when one part is coarse or fine, all are equally so, so, therefore, coarseness of skin and hair indicate a coarse-grained brain, and coarseness of mind; yet since coarseness indicates power, such persons usually possess a great deal of character of some kind. Hence dark-skinned nations are behind light-haired in all the improvements of the age, and the higher finer manifestations of humanity. So, too, dark-haired persons, like Webster are frequently possessed of great power, yet lack the finer and more delicate shadings of sensibility and purity. Coarse black hair and skin, or coarse red hair and face, indicate powerful animal propensities, together with corresponding strength of character; while fine and light hair indicate quick susceptibilities, together with purity, refinement, and good taste. Fine dark or brown hair, indicates a combination of exquisite susceptibilities with great strength of character; while auburn-colored hair, and a florid countenance, indicate the highest order of exquisiteness and intensity of feeling, yet with corresponding purity of character and love of virtue, together with the highest susceptibilities of enjoyment and suffering. And the intermediate colors and textures indicate intermediate mentalities. Coarse-haired persons should never turn dentists or clerks, but should seek some out-door employment; and would be better contented with rough, hard work than a light or sedentary occupation, although mental and sprightly occupations would serve to refine and improve them; while dark and fine-haired persons may choose purely intellectual occupations, and become lecturers or writers with fair prospects of success. Red-haired persons should seek out-door employment, for they require a great amount of air and exercise; while those who have light, fine hair, should choose occupations involving taste and mental acumen, yet take bodily exercise enough to tone and vigorate their system.

Generally, whenever skin, hair, or features are fine or coarse, the others are equally so. Yet some inherit fineness from one parent, and coarseness from the other, while the color of the eye generally corresponds with that of the skin, and expresses character. Light eyes indicate warmth of feeling, and dark eyes power.

The mere expression of eye conveys precise ideas of the existing and predominant states of the mentality and physiology. As long as the constitution remains unimpaired, the eye is clear and bright, but becomes languid and soulless in proportion as the brain has been enfeebled. Wild, erratic persons, have a half-crazed expression of eye, while calmness, benignancy, intelligence, purity, sweetness, love, lasciviousness, anger, and all the other mental affections, express themselves quite as distinctly in the eye as voice, or any other mode.

18.—PHYSIOGNOMY.

Jackson Davis well remarked that, in the spirit land, conversation is carried on mainly, not by words, but by EXPRESSION OF COUNTENANCE—that spirits LOOK their thoughts and motions, rather than talk them. Certain it is that the countenance discloses a greater amount of thought and feeling, together with their nicer shades and phases, than words can possibly communicate. Whether we will or no, we cannot HELP revealing the innermost recesses of our souls in our faces. By what means is this effected? Clairvoyants say by magnetic centres, called poles; each physical and mental organ has its pole stationed in a given part of the face, so that, when such organ becomes active, it influences such poles, and contracts facial muscles, which express the corresponding emotions. That there exists an intimate relation between the stomach and one part of the face, the lungs and another, etc., is proved by the fact that consumptive patients always have a hectic flush on the cheek, just externally from the lower portion of the nose, while inactive lungs cause paleness, and healthy ones give the rosy cheek; and that dyspeptic patients are always lank and thin opposite the double teeth, while those whose digestion is good, are full between the corners of the mouth and lower portion of the ears. Since, therefore, SOME of the states of some of the internal organs express themselves in the face, of course every organ of the body must do the same—the magnetic pole of the heart beginning in the chin. Those whose circulation is vigorous, have broad and rather prominent chins; while those who are small and narrow-chinned have feeble hearts; and thus all the other internal organs have their magnetic poles in various parts of the face.

In like manner have all the PHRENOLOGICAL organs. In 1841, Dr. Sherwood, La Roy Sunderland, and O. S. Fowler, aided by a magnetic subject, located the poles of most of the phrenological and physiological organs, some of which were as follows: Acquisitiveness on each side of the middle portion of the nose, at its junction with the cheek, causing breadth of nose in proportion to the money-grasping instincts, while a narrow nose indicated a want of the speculative turn. Firmness is in the upper lip, midway between its edge and the nose, giving length, prominence, and a compression of the upper lip. Hence, when we would exhort to determined perseverance, we say, "Keep a stiff upper lip." Self-Esteem has its pole externally from that of Firmness, and between the outer portion of the nose and the mouth, causing a fullness, as if a quid of tobacco were under the upper lip. The affections were described as having their poles in the edges of the lips, and hence the philosophy of kissing. The pole of Mirthfulness is located externally, and above the outer corners of the mouth, and hence the drawing up of these corners in laughter. Approbativeness has its pole directly outward from these corners, and hence the approbative laugh does not turn the corners of the mouth upward, but draws them straight back, or outwardly. Like locations were assigned to nearly all the other organs. That physiognomy has its science—that fixed and absolute relations exist between the phrenological organs and given portions of the face is not a matter of question. The natural language of the organs, as seen in the attitudes of the head, indicate not only the presence of large and active organs, but also the signs of their deficiency. Self-Esteem throws the head upward and backward toward the seat of its organ; Approbativeness, back and toward the side Philoprogenitiveness, directly back, but not upward;

Firmness draws the head up, in a stiff, perpendicular position; Individuality thrusts the head forward toward its organ, and gives the man a staring, gazing aspect; small Self-Esteem lets the head droop forward. Man was made both to disclose his own character, and to read that of others. Than this form of knowledge, none is more inviting or useful. Hence God has caused the inherent character of every living being and thing to gush out through every organ of the body, and every avenue of the soul; and also created in both brute and man a character-reading faculty, to take intuitive cognizance of the mental operations. Nor will she let any one lie, any more than lie herself, but compels all to carry the flag of their character at their mast-heads, so that all acquainted with the signs may see and read. If we attempt deception, the very effort convicts us. If all nature's signs of character were fully understood, all could read not only all the main characters of all they see, but even most thoughts and feelings passing in the mind for the time being—a gift worth more than Astor's millions.

19.—REDNESS AND PALENESS OF FACE.

Thus far our remarks have appertained to the constant colors of the face, yet those colors are often diversified or changed for the time being.

Thus, at one time, the whole countenance will be pale, at another, very red; each of which indicates the existing states of body and mind. Or thus; when the system is in a perfectly healthy state, the whole face will be suffused with the glow of health and beauty, and have a red, but never an inflamed aspect; yet any permanent injury of health, which prostrates the bodily energies, will change this florid complexion into dullness of countenance, indicating that but little blood comes to the surface or flows to the head and a corresponding stagnation of the physical and mental powers. Yet, after a time, this dullness frequently gives way to a fiery redness; not the floridness of health, but the redness of inflammation and false excitement, which indicates a corresponding depreciation of the mental faculties. Very red-faced persons, so far from being the most healthy, are frequently the most diseased, and are correspondingly more animal and sensual in character; because physiological inflammation irritates the propensities more, relatively, than the moral and intellectual faculties, though it may, for the time being, increase the latter also. When the moral and intellectual faculties greatly predominate over the animal, such redness of the face may not cause coarse animality, because while it heightens the animal nature, it also increases the intellectual and moral, which, being the larger, hold them in check, but when the animal about equals the moral and intellectual, this inflammation evinces a greater increase of animality than intellectuality and morality. Gross sensualists, and depraved sinners, generally have a fiery, red countenance. Stand aloof from them, for their passions are all on fire, ready to ignite and explode on provocations so slight that a healthy physiology would scarcely notice them. This point can hardly be more fully intelligible; but let readers note the difference between a healthy floridness of face, and the fiery redness of drunkards, debauchees, meat-eaters, etc. Nor does an inflamed physiology merely increase the animal nature, but gives a far more *depraved* and sensual cast to it, thus doubly increasing the tendency to depravity.

20.—HEALTH AND DISEASE AS AFFECTING MENTALITY.

Health and disease affects the mind as much as body. Virtue, goodness, etc., are only the healthy or normal exercise of our various faculties, while depravity and sin are only the sickly exercise of these same organs. Holiness and moral excellence, as well as badness, depend far less upon the relative SIZE of the phrenological organs, than upon their DIRECTION or tone and character, and this depends upon the STATE OF THE BODY. Or thus; a healthy physiology tends to produce a healthy action of the phrenological organs, which is virtue and happiness; while an unhealthy physiology produces that sickly exercise of the mental faculties, especially of the animal propensities, which constitutes depravity and produces misery. Hence those phrenologists who look exclusively to the predominant SIZE of the animal organs, for vicious manifestations, and regard their average size as indicative of virtue, have this great lesson to learn, that health of body produces health of mind and purity of feelings, while all forms of bodily disease, in the very nature of things, tend to corrupt the feelings and deprave the soul. While, therefore, phrenologists should scrutinize the size of organs closely, they should observe the STATE OF HEALTH much more minutely, for most of their errors are explainable on this ground: that the organs described produced vicious inclinations, not because they were so large, but because they were physically SICK, and hence take on a morally DEFORMED mode of action. Phrenologists, look ye well to these points, more fully explained in our other phrenological works.

SECTION II.

PHRENOLOGICAL CONDITIONS AS INDICATING CHARACTER.

21.—DEFINITION AND PROOF.

PHRENOLOGY points out those relations established by nature between given developments and conditions of BRAIN and corresponding manifestations of MIND. Its simple yet comprehensive definition is this: every faculty of the mind is manifested by means of particular portions of the BRAIN called its organs, the size of which, other things being equal, is proportionate to its power of function. For example: it teaches that parental love is manifested by one organ, or portion of the brain; appetite by another, reason by a third, etc., which are large the stronger these corresponding mental powers.

Are, then, particular portions of the brain larger or smaller in proportion as particular mental characteristics are stronger or weaker? Our short-hand answer is illustrated by the following anecdote. A Mr. Juror was once summoned to attend court, but died before its sitting. It therefore devolved upon Mr. Simple to state to the court the reason of his non-appearance. Accordingly, when Mr. Juror's name was called, Mr. Simple responded, "May it please the court, I have twenty-one reasons why Mr. Juror is not in attendance. The first is, he is DEAD. The second is—" "That ONE will answer," responded the judge. "One such reason is amply sufficient." But few of the many proofs that Phrenology is true will here be stated, yet those few are DECISIVE.

First. THE BRAIN IS THE ORGAN OF THE MIND. This is assumed, because too universally admitted to require proof.

Secondly. Is the brain, then, a SINGLE organ, or is it a bundle of organs? Does the WHOLE brain think, remember, love, hate, etc.; or does one portion reason, another worship, another love money, etc.? This is the determining point. To decide it affirmatively, establishes Phrenology; negatively, overthrows it. It is proved by the following facts.

THE EXERCISE OF DIFFERENT FUNCTIONS SIMULTANEOUSLY.—We can walk, think talk remember, love, and many other things all TOGETHER.

—the mind being, in this respect, like a stringed instrument, with several strings vibrating at a time, instead of like a flute which stops the preceding sound when it commences succeeding ones; whereas, if it were a single organ, it must stop thinking the instant it began to talk, could not love a friend and express that love at the same time, and could do but one thing at once.

MONOMANIA.—Since mental derangement is caused only by cerebral disorder, if the brain were a single organ, the WHOLE mind must be sane or insane together; whereas most insane persons are deranged only on one or two points, a conclusive proof of the plurality of the brain and mental faculties.

DIVERSITY OF TALENT, or the fact that some are remarkable for sense, but poor in memory, or the reverse; some forgetting names, but remembering faces; some great mechanics, but poor speakers, or the reverse; others splendid natural singers, but no mechanics, etc., etc., conducts us to a similar conclusion.

INJURIES OF THE BRAIN furnish still more demonstrative proof. If Phrenology be true, to wound and inflame Tune, for example, would create a singing disposition; Veneration, a praying desire; Cautiousness, groundless fears; and so of all the other organs. And thus it is. Nor can this class of facts be evaded. They abound in all phrenological works, especially periodicals, and drive and clench the nail of proof.

COMPARATIVE PHRENOLOGY, or the perfect coincidence existing between the developments and characters of animals, constitutes the highest proof of all. Since man and brute are fashioned upon one great model, those same great optical laws governing the vision of both, that same principle of muscular contraction which enables the eagle to soar aloft beyond our vision, and the whale to furrow and foam the vasty deep, and enabling man to walk forth in the conscious pride of his strength, and thus of all their other common functions; of course, if man is created in accordance with phrenological laws, brutes must also be; and the reverse. If, then, this science is true of either, it must be true of both; must pervade all forms of organization. What, then, are the facts?

Phrenology locates the animal propensities at the SIDES of the head, between and around the ears; the social affections in its BACK and lower portion; the aspiring faculties in its CROWN; the moral on its TOP; and the intellectual on the FOREHEAD; the perceptives, which, related to matter, OVER THE EYES; and the reflectives in the UPPER part of the forehead. (See cut No. 14.)

Now since brutes possess at least only weak moral and reflective faculties, they should, if Phrenology were true, have little top head, and thus it is. Not one of all the following drawings of animals, have much brain in either the reflective or moral region. Almost all their mentality consists of the ANIMAL PROPENSITIES, and nearly all their brain is BETWEEN and

AROUND THEIR EARS, just where, according to Phrenology, it should be. Yet the skulls of all human beings rise high above the eyes and ears, and are long on top, that is, have intellectual and moral ORGANS, as we know they possess these mental ELEMENTS. Comparing the accompanying human

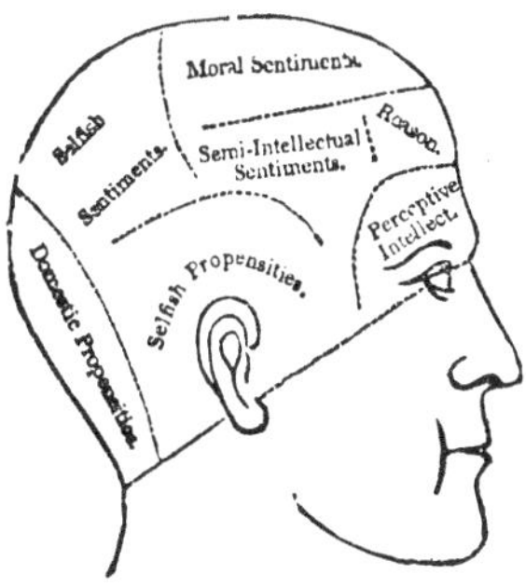

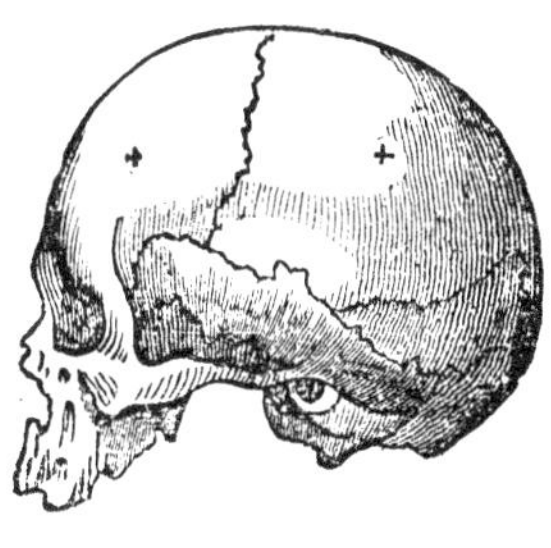

No. 14. GROUPING OF ORGANS. No. 15. HUMAN SKULL

skull with those of brutes, thus those of snakes, frogs, turtles, alligators, etc., slope straight back from the nose; that is, have almost no moral or

No. 16. SNAKE.

No. 17. TURTLE.

intellectual organs; tigers, dogs, lions, etc., have a little more, yet how insignificant compared with man, while monkeys are between them in these organs and their faculties. Here, then, is INDUCTIVE proof of Phrenology as extensive as the whole brute creation on the one hand, contrasted with the entire human family on the other.

Again, Destructiveness is located by Phrenology over the ears, so as to render the head wide in proportion as this organ is developed. Accordingly, all carnivorous animals should be wide-headed at the ears; all herbivorous, narrow. And thus they are, as seen in tigers, hyenas, bears, cats, foxes, ichneumons, etc. compared with rabbits, sheep etc. (Cuts 18, 19, 20, 21, 22, 23, 24, 25, 26, 27, 28, 29, and 30).

DESTRUCTIVENESS LARGE.

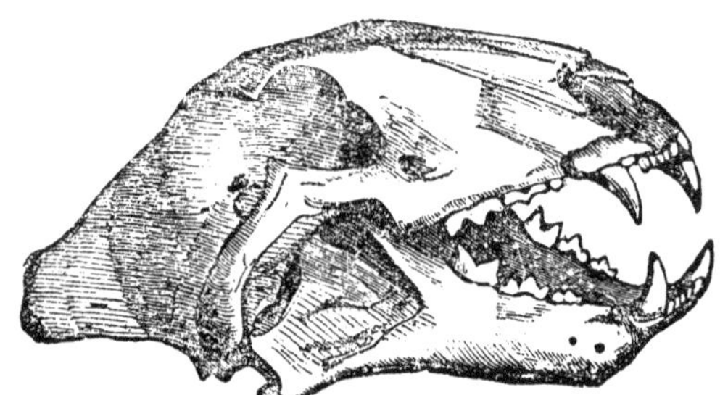

No. 18. TIGER—SIDE VIEW.

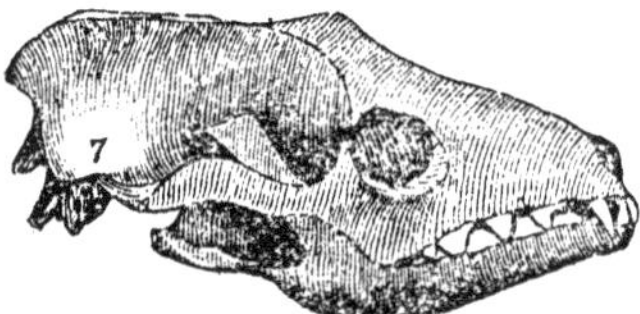

No. 19. HYENA—SIDE VIEW. No. 20. HYENA—BACK VIEW

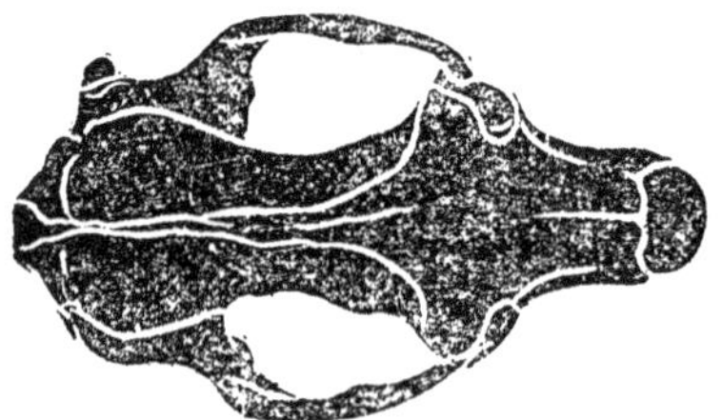

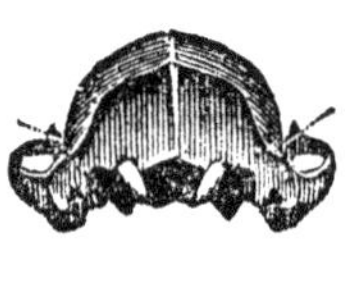

No. 21. BEAR—TOP VIEW. No. 22. BEAR—BACK VIEW

DESTRUCTIVENESS SMALL.

No. 23. SHEEP—TOP VIEW No. 24. RABBIT—SIDE VIEW

To large Destructiveness, in cats, foxes, ichneumons, etc., add large SECRETIVENESS, both in character and head.

SECRETIVENESS AND DESTRUCTIVENESS BOTH LARGE.

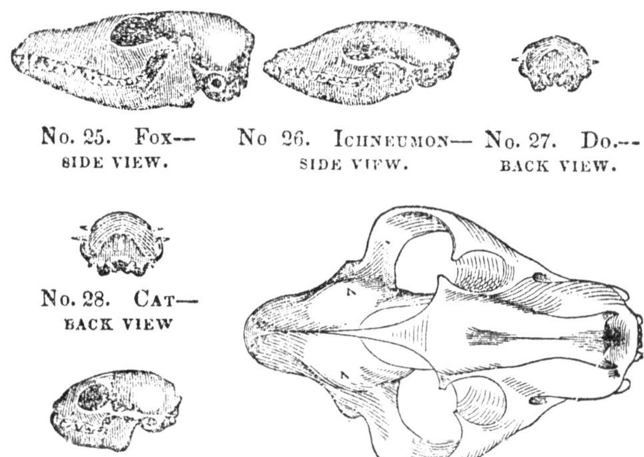

No. 25. FOX—SIDE VIEW.

No. 26. ICHNEUMON—SIDE VIEW.

No. 27. DO.—BACK VIEW.

No. 28. CAT—BACK VIEW.

No. 29. CAT—SIDE VIEW.

No. 30. LION—TOP VIEW.

Fowls, in like manner, correspond perfectly in head and character. Thus, owls, hawks, eagles, etc., have very wide heads, and ferocious dispositions; while hens, turkeys, etc., have narrow heads, and little Destructiveness in character (cuts 31, 32, and 33).

DESTRUCTIVENESS LARGE AND SMALL.

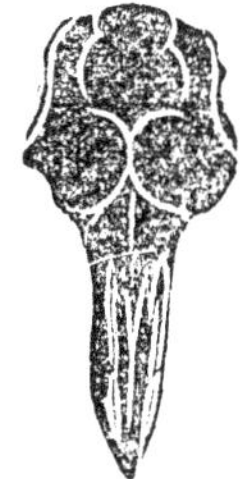

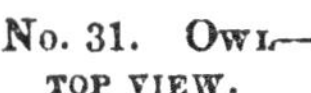

No. 31. OWL—TOP VIEW.

No. 32. HAWK—TOP VIEW.

No. 33. HEN—TOP VIEW.

SECRETIVENESS AND CAUTIOUSNESS LARGE.

No 34. Crow.—

The crow (cut 34) has very large Secretiveness and Cautiousness in the head, as he is known to have in character.

Monkeys, too, bear additional testimony to the truth of phrenological science. They possess, in character, strong perceptive powers, but weak reflectives, and powerful propensities, with feeble moral elements. Accordingly they are full over the eyes, but slope straight back at the reasoning and moral faculties, while the propensities engross most of their brain.

No. 35. Intelligent Monkey.

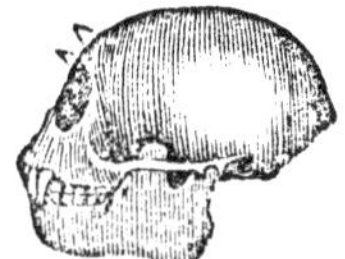

No. 36. Do.—side view

SOME MORAL AND REFLECTIVE BRAIN.

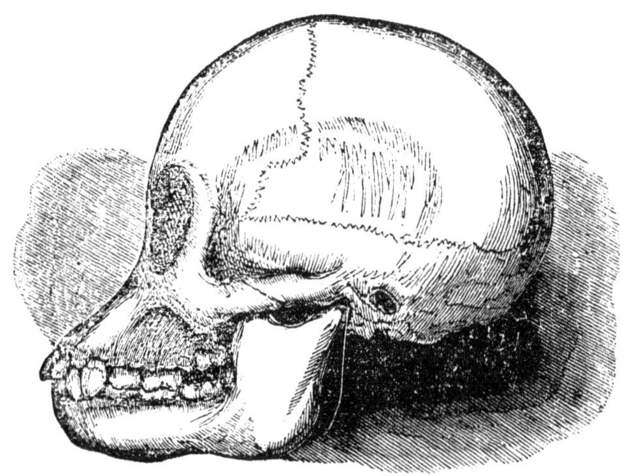

No. 37 Jack, the Orang-outang.

The ORANG-OUTANG has more forehead than any other animal, both perceptive and reflective, with some moral sentiments, and accordingly is called the "half-reasoning man," its Phrenology corresponding perfectly with its character.

PERCEPTIVES LARGER THAN REFLECTIVES.

No. 38. AFRICAN HEAD.

THE VARIOUS RACES also accord with phrenological science. Thus, Africans generally have full perceptives, and large Tune and Language, but retiring Causality, and accordingly are deficient in reasoning capacity, yet have excellent memories and lingual and musical powers.

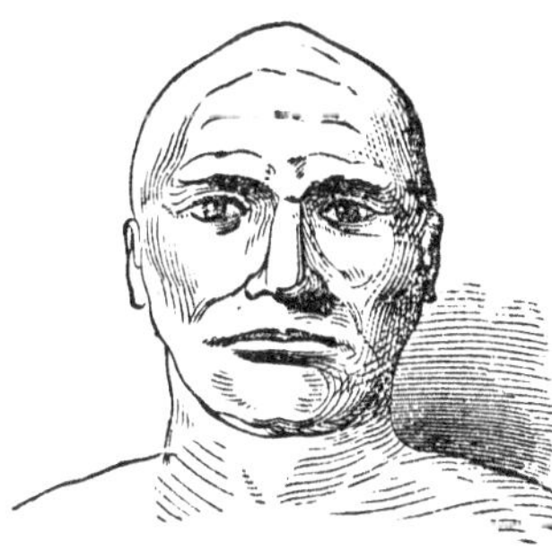

No. 39. INDIAN CHIEF.

Indians possess extraordinary strength of the propensities and perceptives, yet have no great moral or inventive power; and, hence, have very wide, round, conical, and rather low heads.

Indian skulls can always be selected from Caucasian, just by these developments; while the Caucasian race is superior in reasoning power and moral elevation to all the other races, and, accordingly, have higher and bolder foreheads, and more elevated and elongated top heads.

Finally, contrast the massive foreheads of all giant-minded men—Bacons, Franklins, Miltons, etc., with idiotic heads.

In short, every human, every brutal head, is constructed throughout strictly on phrenological principles. Ransack air, earth, and water and not one palpable exception ever has been, ever can be adduced This

LARGE AND SMALL INTELLECTS.

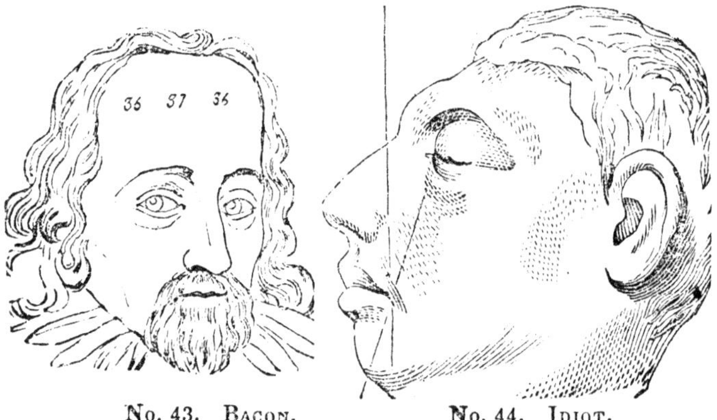

No. 43. BACON. No. 44. IDIOT.

WHOLE-SOUL view of this science precludes the possibility of mistake. Phrenology is therefore a PART AND PARCEL OF NATURE—A UNIVERSAL FACT.

THE PHILOSOPHY OF PHRENOLOGY.

All truth bears upon its front unmistakable evidence of its divine origin, in its philosophical consistency, fitness, and beauty, whereas all untruth is grossly and palpably deformed. All truth, also, harmonizes with all other truth, and conflicts with all error, so that to ascertain what is true, and detect what is false, is perfectly easy, Apply this test, intellectual reader to one after another of the doctrines, as presented in this science. But enough on this point of proofs. Let us proceed to its illustration.

22.—PHRENOLOGICAL SIGNS OF CHARACTER.

The brain is not only the organ of the mind, the dome of thought, the palace of the soul, but is equally the organ of the *body*, over which it exerts an all-potent influence for good or ill, to weaken or stimulate, to kill or make alive. In short, the brain is the organ of the body in general, and of all its organs in particular. It sends forth those nerves which keep muscles, liver, bowels, and all the other bodily organs in a high or low state of action; and, more than all other causes, invites or repels disease, prolongs or shortens life, and treats the body as its galley-slave. Hence, healthy cerebral action is indispensable to bodily health. Hence, too, we walk or work so much more easily and efficiently when we take an *interest* in what we do. Therefore those who would be happy or talented must first and mainly keep their BRAIN vigorous and healthy.

The brain is subdivided into two hemispheres, the right and left, by the falciform process of the dura mater, a membrane which dips down one to two inches into the brain, and runs from the root of the nose over to the nape of the neck. This arrangement renders all the phrenological organs DOUBLE. Thus, as there are two eyes, ears, etc., that when one is diseased, the other can carry forward the functions, so there are two lobes to each phrenological organ, one on each side. The brain is divided thus: the feelings occupy that portion commonly covered by the hair, while the forehead is occupied by the intellectual organs. These greater divisions are subdivided into the animal brain, located between and around the ears; the aspiring faculties, which occupy the crown of the head; the moral and religious sentiments, which occupy the top; the physico-perceptives, located over the eyes; and the reflectives, in the upper portion of the forehead. The predominance of these respective groups produces both particular shapes, and corresponding traits of character. Thus, when the head projects far back behind the ears, hanging over and downward in the occipital region, it indicates very strong domestic ties and social affections, a love of home, its relations and endearments, and a corresponding high capacity of being happy in the family, and of making the family happy. Very wide and round heads, on the contrary, indicate strong animal and selfish propensities, while thin, narrow heads, indicate a corresponding want of selfishness and animality. A head projecting far up at the crown, indicates an aspiring, self-elevating disposition, proudness of character, and a desire to be and to do something great; while the flattened crown indicates a want of ambition, energy, and aspiration. A head high, long, and wide upon the top, but narrow between the ears, indicates Causality, moral virtue, much practical goodness, and a corresponding elevation of character; while a low or narrow top head indicates a corresponding deficiency of these humane and religious susceptibilities. A head wide at the upper part of the temples, indicates a corresponding desire for personal perfection, together with a love of the beautiful and refined, while narrowness in this region evinces a want of taste, with much coarseness of feeling. Fullness over the eyes indicates excellent practical judgment of matters and things appertaining to property, science, and nature in general; while narrow, straight eyebrows, indicate poor practical judgment of matter, its quality, relations, and uses. Fullness from the root of the nose upward, indicates great practical talent, love of knowledge, desire to see, and ability to do to advantage, together with sprightliness of mind; while a hollow in the middle of the forehead indicates want of memory and inability to show off to advantage. A bold, high forehead, indicates strong reasoning capabilities, while a retiring forehead indicates less soundness, but more availability of talent.

23.—THE NATURAL LANGUAGE OF THE FACULTIES.

Phrenology shows that every faculty, when active, throws head and body in the direction of that faculty. Thus. intellect, in the fore part of the head, throws it directly forward, and produces a forward hanging motion of the head. Hence intellectual men never carry their heads

No. 40. WASHINGTON IRVING.

backward and upward, but always forward; and logical speakers move their heads in a straight line, usually forward, toward their audience; while vain speakers carry their heads backward. Perceptive intellect, when active, throws out the chin and lower portions of the face; while reflective intellect causes the upper portion of the forehead to hang forward, and draws in the chin, as in the engravings of Franklin, Webster, and other great thinkers Benevolence throws the head and body slightly forward, leaning toward the object which excites its sympathy; while Veneration causes a low bow, which, the world over, is a token of respect; yet, when Veneration is exercised toward the Deity, as in devout prayer, it throws the head UPWARD; and, as we use intellect at the same time, the head is generally directed forward. Ideality throws the head slightly forward, and to one side, as in Washington Irving, a man as gifted in taste and imagination as almost any living writer; and, in his portraits, his finger rests upon this faculty; while in Sterne, the finger rests upon Mirthfulness. Very firm men stand straight up and down, inclining not a hair's breadth forward or backward, or to the right or left; hence the expression, "He is an up-and-down man." And this organ is located exactly on a line with the body. Self-Esteem, located in the back and upper portion of the head, throws the head and body upward and backward. Large feeling, pompous persons, always walk in a very dignified,

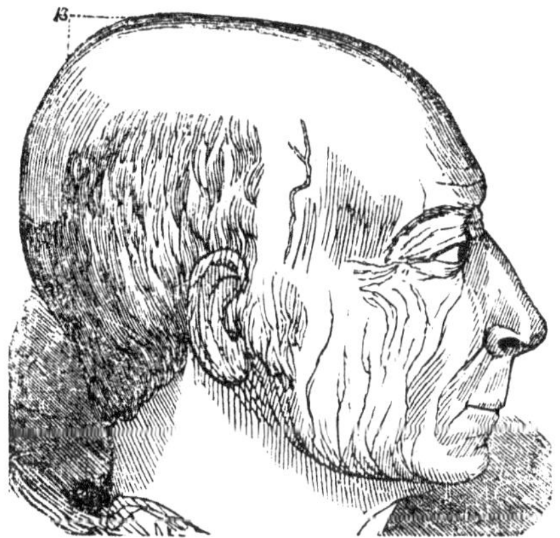

No. 45. A CONCEITED SIMPLETON.

majestic posture, and always throw their heads in the direction of Self-Esteem; whilst approbative persons throw their heads backward, but to the one side or both. The difference between these two organs being comparatively slight, only the practical Phrenologist's eye can perfectly distinguish them.

There is, moreover, a natural language of money-loving, and that is a leaning forward and turning of the head to one side, as if in ardent pursuit of something, and ready to grasp it with outstretched arms; while Alimentiveness, situated lower down, hugs itself down to the dainty dish with the greediness of an epicure, better seen than described. The shake of the head is the natural language of Combativeness, and means no, or I resist you. Those who are combating earnestly upon politics, or any other subject, shake the head more or less violently, according to the power of the combative feeling, but always shake it slightly inclining *backwards;* while Destructiveness, inclining forward, causes a shaking of the head slightly forward, and turning to one side. When a person who threatens you shakes his head violently, and holds it pertially backward, and to one side, never fear—he is only barking; but whenever he inclines his head to one side, and shakes it violently, that dog will bite, whether possessed of two legs or four. The social affections are located in the *back* part of the head; and, accordingly, woman being more loving than man, when not under the influence of the other faculties, usually inclines her head backward toward the neck; and when she kisses children, and those whom she loves, always turns the head directly backward, and rolls it from side to side, on the back of the neck. Thus it is that all the various postures assumed by it individually, are expressive of the present or the permanent activity of their respective faculties.

No. 44. Jonathan Edwards.

24.—ORGANIC TONE OR QUALITY OF BRAIN.

This condition modifies character more than any other. It is, indeed, the summing up of all. It consists of two kinds, original and acquired. The former, inherited from parents, embraces the pristine vigor and power with which the life principle was started, and gives what we will call SNAP; while the latter embraces the *existing* states of the organism as affected by health or debility, artificial habits—such as dyspeptic and other affections, caused by injurious qualities and quantities of food, by artificial stimulants, as tea, coffee, tobacco, or alcoholic drinks—the deranged or healthy states of the nervous system; too much or too little exercise, labor, sleep, breath, etc., etc.; and whatever other conditions are embraced in health and disease, or in any way affect them. Of course, the parental may be good, but acquired poor, or the reverse, according as the subject is strengthening or enfeebling, building up or breaking down his physical constitution, by correct or erroneous physiological habits

Yet, in most persons, the parental is many hundred per cent. better than the acquired

PARENTAL GOOD, OR VERY GOOD, gives corresponding innate vigor and energy, or that heart and bottom which wears like iron, and bends, willow-like, without breaking, and performs more with a given size, than greater size, and less inherent "snap;" and gives thoroughness and edge to the mentality, just as good steel, well tempered, does to the tool

PARENTAL FAIR gives a good share of the presiding qualities, yet nothing remarkable; with acquired good endures and accomplishes much; without it, soon breaks down.

No. 45. EMERSON, AN IDIOT.

PARENTAL POOR leaves its subject poorly organized, bodily and mentally, and proportionally low in the creative scale.

ACQUIRED GOOD enables whatever of life power there is, to perform all of which it is capable; with parental good, furnishes a full supply of vital power, and that activity which works it all up in mental or physical labor. With parental very good, puts forth a most astonishing amount of effort, and endures wonders without injury; possesses remarkable clearness and wholeness of mind; thinks and feels directly to the purpose; gives point and cogency to every thing; and confers a superior amount of healthy intellectuality, morality, and mentality, in general.

ACQUIRED FAIR, with parental average, gives fair natural talents, and mental and physical vigor, yet nothing remarkable; will lead a commonplace life, and possess an every-day charcter, memory, etc.; will not set the world on fire, nor be insignificant, but, with cultivation, will do well.

ACQUIRED POOR will be unable to put forth its inherent power; is weak and inefficient, though desirous of doing something; with parental good, may take hold resolutely, but soon tires, and finds it impossible to sustain that powerful action with which it naturally commences.

25.—STATES OF THE NERVOUS SYSTEM.

A good nervous condition enables its possessor to put forth sound and healthy mental and physical efforts; gives a calm, quiet, happy, contented frame of mind, and a strong tendency to enjoy every thing—even the bad; makes the most of life's joys, and the least of its sorrows: confers full possession of all its innate powers; and predisposes to a right exercise of all the faculties.

Disordered nerves produce an irritated, craving, dissatisfied state of mind, and a tendency to depravity in some of its forms, with a half paralyzed, lax, inefficient state of mind and body.

26.—SIZE OF HEAD AS INFLUENCING CHARACTER.

Size of head and organs, other things being equal, is the great phrenological condition. Though tape measurements, taken around the head, from Individuality to Philoprogenitiveness, give some idea of the size of brain, the fact that some heads are round, others long, some low, and others high, so modifies these measurements that they do not convey any very correct idea of the actual quantity of brain. Yet these measurements range somewhat as follows. Least size of adults compatible with fair talents, 20¼; 20¾ to 21¼, moderate; 21¼ to 22, average; 22 to 22¾, full; 22¾ to 23¾, large; above 23¾, very large. Female heads, ½ to ¾ below these averages.

Large.—One having a large sized brain, with activity *average*, will *possess* considerable energy of intellect and feeling, yet seldom manifest it, unless it is brought out by some powerful stimulus, and will be rather too indolent to exert, especially his *intellect:* with activity *full*, will be endowed with an uncommon amount of the mental power, and be capable of doing a good deal, yet require considerable to awaken him to that vigorous effort of mind of which he is capable; if his powers are not called out by circumstances, and his organs of practical intellect are only average or full, he may pass through life without attracting notice, or manifesting more than an ordinary share of talent: but if the perceptive faculties are strong, or very strong, and his natural powers put in vigorous requisition, he will manifest a vigor and energy of intellect and feeling quite above mediocrity; be adequate to undertakings which demand originality of mind and force of character, yet, after all, be rather indolent: with activity *great, or very great*, will combine great *power* of mind with great activity; exercise a commanding influence over those minds with which he comes in contact; when he enjoys, will enjoy intensely, and when he suffers, suffer equally so; be susceptible of strong excitement, and, with the organs of the propelling powers, and of practical intellect, large or very large, will possess all the mental capabilities for conducting a large business; for rising to eminence, if not to pre-eminence; and discover great force of character and power of intellect and feeling: with activity *moderate*, when powerfully excited, will evince considerable energy of intellect and feeling, yet be too indolent and too sluggish to do much; lack clearness and force of idea, and intenseness of feeling; unless literally driven to it, will not be likely to be much or to do much, and yet actually *possess* more vigor of mind, and energy of feeling, than he will manifest; with activity small, or very small, will border upon idiocy.

Very Large.—One having a very large head, with activity *average* or *full*, on great occasions, or when his powers are thoroughly roused, will be truly great; but upon ordinary occasions, will seldom manifest any remarkable amount of mind or feeling, and perhaps pass through life with the credit of being a person of good natural abilities and judgment, yet nothing more; with *great* activity and strength, and large intellectual organs, will be a natural genius, endowed with very superior powers of mind and vigor of intellect; and, even though deprived of the advantages of education, his natural talents will surmount all obstacles, and make him truly talented; with activity *very great*, and the organs of practical intellect and of the propelling powers large, or very large, will possess the first order of natural abilities; manifest a clearness and force of intellect which will astonish the world, and a power of feeling which will carry all before him; and, with proper cultivation, enable him to become a bright star in the firmament of intellectual greatness, upon which coming ages may gaze with delight and astonishment. His mental enjoyment will be most exquisite, and his sufferings equally keen.

Full.—One having a full-sized brain, with activity *great, or very great*, and the organs of practical intellect and of the propelling powers large, or very large, although he will not possess *greatness* of intellect, nor a deep, strong mind, will be very clever; have considerable talent, and that so distributed that it will show to be *more* than it really is; is capable of being a good scholar, doing a fine business, and, with advantages and application, of distinguishing himself somewhat; yet he is inadequate to a great undertaking; cannot sway an extensive influence, nor be really great; with activity *full, or average*, will do only tolerably well, and manifest only a common share of talent; with activity *moderate, or small*, will neither be nor do much worthy of notice.

Average, with activity great, manifests a quick, clear, sprightly mind and off-hand talents; and is capable of doing a fair business, especially if the stamina is good; with activity *very great*, and the organs of the propelling powers and of practical intellect large, or very large, is capable of doing a good business, and may pass for a man of fair talent, yet will not be original or profound; will be quick of perception; have a good practical understanding; will do well *in his sphere*, yet never manifest greatness, and out of his sphere, be common-place; with activity only *average*, will discover only an ordinary amount of intellect; be inadequate to any important undertaking; yet, in a small sphere, or one that requires only a mechanical routine of business, may do well; with *moderate or small* activity, will hardly have common sense.

Moderate.—One with a head of only moderate size, combined with *great* or *very great activity,* and the organs of the propelling powers and of practical intellect large, will possess a tolerable share of intellect, yet be more showy than sound; with others to plan for and direct him, will execute to advantage, yet be unable to do much alone; will have a very active mind, and be quick of perception, yet, after all, have a contracted intellect; possess only a small mental calibre, and lack momentum, both of mind and character; with activity only *average, or fair,* will have but a moderate *amount* of intellect, and even this scanty allowance will be too sluggish for action, so that he will neither suffer nor enjoy much; with activity *moderate or small,* will be idiotic.

Small or Very Small.—One with a small or very small head, no matter what may be the activity of his mind, will be incapable of much intellectual effort; of comprehending even easy subjects; or of experiencing much pain or pleasure; in short, will be mentally imbecile.

47.—SIZE OF BRAIN AS AFFECTING MENTALITY.

Most great men have great heads. Webster's head measures over 24 inches, and Clay's considerably above 23; and this is about Van Buren's size; Chief Justice Gibson's, the greatest jurist in Pennsylvania, 24½; Napoleon's reached nearly or quite to 24, his hat passing easily over the head of one of his officers, which measured 23½; and Hamilton's hat passed over the head of a man whose head measured 23½. Burke's head was immense, so was Jefferson's; while Franklin's hat passed over the ears of a 24-inch head. Small and average sized heads often astonish us by their brilliancy and learning, and, perhaps, eloquence, yet they fail in that commanding greatness which impresses and sways mind. The phrenological law is, that size, other things being equal, is a measure of power; yet these other conditions, such as activity, power of motive, health, physiological habits, etc., increase or diminish the mentality, even more than size.

SECTION III.

ANALYSIS AND COMBINATIONS OF THE FACULTIES

---

1. AMATIVENESS.

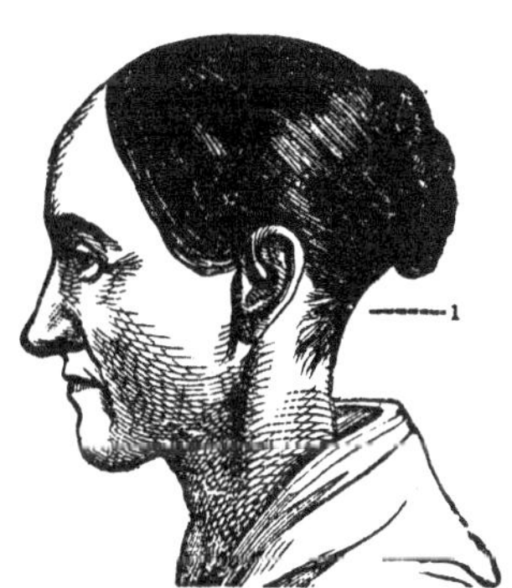

No. 45. Large. No. 46. Small.

Conjugal love; attachment to the opposite sex; desire to love, be loved, and marry; adapted to perpetuate the race. It causes those mutual attractions which exist between the sexes; creates love; induces marriage; eventuates in offspring; renders woman winning, persuasive, urbane, affectionate, loving, and lovely; and develops all the feminine charms and graces; and makes man noble in feeling and bearing; elevated in aspiration; tender and bland in manner; affectionate toward woman; pure in feeling; highly susceptible to female charms; and clothes him with that dignity, power, and persuasiveness, which accompanies the masculine. Perverted, it occasions a grossness and vulgarity in expression and action; licentiousness in all its forms; a feverish state of mind; and depraves all the other propensities; treats the other sex merely as a minister to passion; now caressing, and now abusing them; and renders the love-feeling every way gross, animal, and depraved.

LARGE.—Is strongly attracted toward the opposite sex; admires and loves their beauty and excellencies; easily wins their affectionate regards, or kindles their love; has many warm friends, if not admirers, among them; loves young and powerfully, and wields a potent influence for good or evil over the destinies of its subject, according as it is well or ill placed; with Adhesiveness and Union for Life large, will mingle pure friendship with devoted love; cannot flourish alone, but must have its matrimonial mate, with whom it will be capable of becoming perfectly identified, and whom it will invest with almost superhuman perfections, by magnifying their charms and overlooking their defects; in the sunshine of whose love it will be perfectly happy, but proportionally miserable without it; with Ideality and the mental temperament large, will experience a fervor and intensity of first love, amounting almost to ecstacy or romance; can marry those only who combine refinement of manners with correspondingly strong attachments; with Philoprogenitiveness and Benevolence also large, will be eminently qualified to enjoy the domestic relations; to be happy in home, and render home happy; with Inhabitiveness also large, will set a high value on house and place long to return home when absent, and consider family and children as the greatest treasures of its being; with large Conscientiousness, will keep the marriage relations inviolate, and regard unfaithfulness as the greatest of sins; with Combativeness large, will defend the objects of its love with great spirit, and resent powerfully any indignity offered to them; with Alimentiveness large, will enjoy eating with the family dearly; with Approbativeness large, cannot endure to be blamed by those it loves; with Cautiousness and Secretiveness large, will express love guardedly, and much less than it experiences; but with Secretiveness small, will show, in every look and action, the full, unveiled feeling of the mind; with Firmness and Self-Esteem large, will sustain interrupted love with fortitude, yet suffer much damage of mind and health therefrom; but with Self-Esteem moderate, will feel crushed and broken down by disappointment; with the moral faculties predominant, can love those only whose moral tone is pure and elevated; with predominant Ideality, and only average intellectual faculties, will prefer those who are showy and gay, to those who are sensible yet less beautiful; but with Ideality less than the intellectual and moral organs, will prefer those who are substantial and valuable more than showy; with Mirthfulness, Time, and Tune, will love dancing, lively society, etc.: p. 57.

VERY LARGE.—Confers the strongest possible inclination to love; exercises an absolute influence over character and conduct; must always have a congenial spirit whom to love, and by whom to be loved; is capable of the highest order of love, and is proportionally beautified thereby; can love with complete devotedness, even under unfavorable circumstances, and has a most important element for conjugal happiness and a matrimonial partner its combinations will be somewhat the same as those under Amativeness large, allowance being made for the increased power of this faculty p. 58.

FULL.—Possesses rather strong susceptibilities of love, and conjugal affinity and unity to a congenial spirit; is capable of much purity, intensity, and cordiality of love; with Adhesiveness and Benevolence large, will render good service in the family; with Secretivness large, will manifest less love than it feels, and show little in promiscuous society; with a highly susceptible temperament, will experience great intensity of love, and evince a good degree of masculine or feminine excellence: p. 59.

AVERAGE.—Is capable of fair sexual attachments, and conjugal love, provided it is properly placed and fully called out; experiences a greater or less degree of love in proportion to its activity; renders the son quite attached to mother and sisters, and fond of female society, and endowed with a fair share of the masculine element, yet not remarkable for its perfection, makes woman quite winning and attractive, yet not particularly susceptible to love; renders the daughter fond of father and brothers, and desirous of the society of men, yet not extremely so; and capable of a fair share of conjugal devotedness under favorable circumstances; combined with an ardent temperament, and large Adhesiveness and Ideality, gives a pure and platonic cast of love, yet cannot assimilate with a coarse temperament, or a dissimilar Phrenology; is refined, and faithful, yet has more friendship than passion; can love those only who are just to its liking; with Cautiousness and Secretiveness large, will express less love than it feels, and that equivocally and by piecemeal, nor then till its loved one is fully committed; with Cautiousness, Approbativeness and Veneration large, and Self-Esteem small, will be diffident in promiscuous society, yet enjoy the company of a select few of the opposite sex; with Adhesiveness, Benevolence, and Conscientiousness large, and Self-Esteem small, will be kind and affectionate in the family, yet not particularly fond of caressing or being caressed; and will do much to make family happy, yet will manifest less fondness and tenderness; with Order, Approbativeness, and Ideality large, will seek in a companion personal neatness and polish of manners; with full intellectual and moral faculties, will base its conjugal attachments in the higher qualities of the affections, rather than their personal attractiveness or strength of passion; but with a commonplace temperament, and not so full moral and intellectual faculties, will be an indifferent companion: p. 56.

MODERATE.—Will be rather deficient, though not palpably so, in the love element: show little desire to caress or be caressed; will love the mental excellences of the other sex more than personal beauty, and find it difficult to sympathize with a conjugal partner, unless the natural harmony between the parties is well-nigh perfect; cares less for marriage, and could live an unmarried life without inconvenience; can love but once, and should marry only the first love, because the love-principle will not be sufficiently strong to overcome the difficulties incident to a second love, or the want of a congenial companion, and find more pleasure in other things than in the matrimonial relations; with an excitable temperament, will experience greater warmth and ardor, than depth and uniformity of love; with Approbativeness large, will soon become alienated from a lover by rebukes and fault-finding; with Adhesiveness and the moral and intellectual faculties large, can become strongly attached to those who are highly moral and intellectual, yet experiences no affinity for any other, and to be happy in marriage, must base it in the higher faculties: p. 59.

SMALL.—Feels little conjugal or sexual love, and desire to marry; is cold, coy, distant, and reserved toward the other sex; experiences but little of the beautifying and elevating influence of love, and should not marry, because incapable of appreciating its relation and making a companion happy: p. 59.

VERY SMALL.—Is passively continent, and almost destitute of love: p. 60.

---

2. PHILOPROGENITIVENESS.

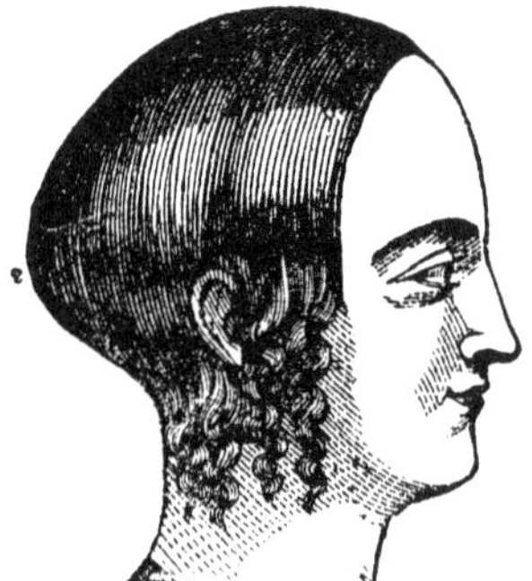

No. 47. LARGE.

No 48. SMALL.

Parental love; attachment to one's own offspring; love of children, pets, and animals generally, especially those young or small; adapted to that infantile condition in which man enters the world, and to children's need of parental care and education. This faculty renders children the richest treasure of their parents; casts into the shade all the toil and expense they cause, and lacerates them with bitter pangs when death or distance tears them asunder. It is much larger in woman than in man; and nature requires mothers to take the principal care of infants. Perverted, it spoils children by excessive fondness, pampering, and humoring.

LARGE.—Loves its own children devotedly; values them above all price; cheerfully endures toil and watching for their sake; forbears with their faults; wins their love; delights to play with them, and cheerfully sacrifices to promote their interests; with Continuity large, mourns long and incessantly over their loss; with Combativeness, Destructiveness, and Self-Esteem large, is kind, yet insists on being obeyed; with Self-Esteem and Destructiveness moderate, is familiar with, and liable to be ruled by them; with Firmness only average, fails to manage them with a steady hand; with Cautiousness large, suffers extreme anxiety if they are sick or in danger; with large moral and intellectual organs, and less Combativeness and Destructiveness, governs them more by moral suasion than physical force—by reason than fear—is neither two strict nor over-indulgent; with Approbativeness large, values their moral character as of the utmost importance; with Veneration and Conscientiousness large, is particularly interested in their moral improvement; with large excitability, Combativeness, and Destructiveness, and only average Firmness, will be, by turns, too indulgent, and over-provoked—will pet them one minute, and punish them the next; with larger Approbativeness and Ideality than intellect, will educate them more for show than usefulness—more fashionably than substantially—and dress them off in the extreme of fashion; with a large and active brain, large moral and intellectual faculties, and Firmness, and only full Combativeness, Destructiveness, and Self-Esteem, is well calculated to teach and manage the young. It renders farmers fond of stock, dogs etc., and women fond of birds, lap-dogs, etc.; girls fond of dolls, and boys of being among horses and cattle; and creates a general interest in young and small animals: p. 62.

VERY LARGE.—Experiences the feeling above described with still greater intensity and power; almost idolizes its children, grieves immeasurably at their loss, and, with large Continuity, refuses to be comforted; with very large Benevolence, and only moderate Destructiveness, cannot bear to see them punished, and, with only moderate Causality, is liable to spoil them by over-indulgence; with large Approbativeness added, indulges parental vanity and conceit; with large Cautiousness and disordered nerves, is always cautioning them, and indulges a world of groundless apprehensions about them with Acquisitiveness moderate, makes them many presents, and lavishes money upon them, but with large Acquisitiveness lays up fortunes for them; with large moral and intellectual organs, is indulgent, yet loves them too well to spoil them, and does his utmost to cultivate their higher faculties: etc., p. 63.

FULL.—Loves its children well, yet not passionately—does much for them, yet not more than is necessary—and with large Combativeness, Destructiveness, and Self-Esteem, is too severe, and makes but little allowance for their faults; but with Benevolence, Adhesiveness, and Conscientiousness large, does and sacrifices much, to supply their wants and render them happy. Its character, however, will be mainly determined by its combinations: p. 63.

AVERAGE.—Loves its own children tolerably well, yet cares but little for those of others; with large Adhesiveness and Benevolence, likes them better as they grow older, yet does and cares little for infants—is not duly tender to them, or forbearing toward their faults, and should cultivate parental fondness, especially if Combativeness, Destructiveness, and Self-Esteem are large, and conscience only moderate: p. 61.

MODERATE.—Is not fond enough of children; cannot bear much from them; fails to please or take good care of them, particularly of infants; cannot endure to hear them cry, or make a noise, or disturb his things; and with an excitable temperament, and large Combativeness, is liable to punish them for trifling offences, find much fault with them, and be sometimes cruel; yet, with Benevolence and Adhesiveness large, may do what is necessary for their comfort: p. 64.

SMALL.—Cares little for its own children, and still less for those of others; and with Combativeness and Destructivness large, is liable to treat them unkindly and harshly, and is utterly unqualified to have charge of them: p. 64.

VERY SMALL.—Has little or no perceptible parental love, or regard for children, but conducts toward them as the other faculties dictate: p 64.

---

3. ADHESIVENESS.

Friendship; social feeling; love of society; desire to congregate, associate, visit, seek company, entertain friends, form and reciprocate attachments, and indulge friendly feelings. When perverted, it forms attachments for the low, vulgar, or vicious, and leads to bad company. Adapted to man's requisition for concert of action, co-partnership, combination, and community of feeling and interest, and is a leading element of his social relations.

LARGE.—Is a warm, cordial, ardent friend; readily forms friendships, and attracts friendly regards in return; must have society of some kind; with Benevolence large, is hospitable, and delights to entertain friends; with Alimentiveness large, loves the social banquet, and sets the best before friends; with Approbativeness large, sets the world by their commendation, but is terribly cut by their rebukes; with the moral faculties large, seeks the society of the moral and elevated, and can enjoy the friendship of no others; with the intellectual faculties large, seeks the friendship of the intelligent; with Language large, and Secretiveness small, talks freely in company; and with Mirthfulness and Ideality also large, is full of fun, and gives a lively, jocose turn to conversation, yet is elevated and refined; with Self-Esteem large, leads off in company, and gives tone and character to others; but with Self-Esteem small, receives character from friends, and, with Imitation large, is liable to copy their faults as well as virtues; with Cautiousness, Secretiveness, and Approbativeness large, is apt to be jealous of regards bestowed upon others, and exclusive in its choice of friends—having a few that are select, rather than many that are common-place; with large Causality and Comparison, loves philosophical conversation, literary societies, etc.; and is every way social and companionable: p. 65.

VERY LARGE.—Loves friends with tenderness, and intense friendship, and will sacrifice almost any thing for their sake; with Amativeness large, is susceptible of the highest order of conjugal love, yet bases that love primarily in friendship; with Combativeness and Destructiveness large, defends friends with great spirit, and resents and retaliates their injuries; with Self-Esteem moderate, takes character from associates; with Acquisitiveness moderate, allows friends the free use of its purse but with Acquisitiveness large, will do, more than give; with Benevolence and Approbativeness moderate, and Acquisitiveness only full, will spend money freely for social gratification; with Self-Esteem and Combativeness large, must be first or nothing; but with only average Combativeness, Destructiveness, and Self-Esteem, large Approbativeness, Benevolence, Conscientiousness, Ideality, Marvellousness, and reasoning organs, will have many friends, and but few enemies—be amiable and universally beloved; with large Eventuality and Language, will remember, with vivid emotions, by-gone scenes of social cheer, and friendly converse; with large reasoning organs, will give good advice to friends, and lay excellent plans for them; with smaller Secretiveness and large moral organs, will not believe ill of friends, and dreads the interruption of friendship as the greatest of calamities, and willingly makes any sacrifice required by friendship, and evinces a perpetual flow of that commingling of soul, and desire to become one with others, which this faculty inspires: p. 65.

FULL.—Makes a sociable, companionable, warm-hearted friend, who will sacrifice much on the altar of friendship, yet offer up friendship on the altar of the stronger passions; with large or very large Combativeness, Destructiveness, Self-Esteem, Approbativeness and Acquisitiveness, will serve self first, and friends afterward; form attachments, and break them, when they conflict with the stronger faculties; with large Secretiveness, and moderate Conscientiousness, will be double-faced, and profess more friendship than possess; with Benevolence large, will cheerfully aid friends, yet it will be more from sympathy than affection; will have a few warm friends, yet only few, but perhaps many speaking acquaintances; and with the higher faculties generally large, will be a true, good friend, yet by no means enthusiastic; many of the combinations under Adhesiveness large, apply to it when full, due allowance being made for its diminished power: p. 66.

AVERAGE.—Is capable of tolerably strong friendships, yet their character is determined by the larger faculties; enjoys present friends, yet sustains their absence; with large Acquisitiveness, places business before friends, and sacrifices them whenever they conflict with money-making; with Benevolence large, is more kind than affectionate, relishes friends, yet sacrifices no great deal for their sake; with Amativeness large, loves the presence of the other sex more than their minds, and experiences less conjugal love than animal passion; with Approbativeness large, breaks friendships when ridiculed or rebuked, and with Secretiveness large, and Conscientiousness only average, cannot be trusted as a friend: p. 64.

MODERATE.—Loves society somewhat, and forms a few, but only few attachments, and these only partial; has more speaking acquaintances than intimate friends; with large Combativeness and Destructiveness, is easily offended with friends, and seldom retains them long; with large Benevolence, will bestow services, and, with moderate Acquisitiveness, money, more readily than affection; and with the selfish faculties strong, takes care of self first, and makes friendship subservient to interest: p. 67.

SMALL.—Thinks and cares little for friends; dislikes copartnership; is cold-hearted, unsocial, and selfish; takes little delight in company, but prefers to be alone; has few friends, and, with large selfish faculties, many enemies, and manifests too little of this faculty to exert a perceptible influence upon character: p. 67.

VERY SMALL.—Is a perfect stranger to friendship: p. 67.

A. UNION FOR LIFE.

Attachment to ONE, and BUT ONE conjugal partner for life. Adapted to the pairing principle in man and animals, and is located between Adhesiveness and Amativeness. Some birds, such as geese, eagles, robins, etc., pair for life, and remain true to their connubial attachment; while hens, turkies, sheep, horses, and neat cattle, associate promiscuously, which shows that it is a faculty distinct from Amativeness and Adhesiveness.

LARGE.—Seeks one, and but one sexual mate; experiences the keenest disappointment when love is interrupted; is perfectly satisfied with the society of that one, and can truly love no other, and retains that love even after its object is dead; may love and marry another, but it will be more from motives of policy than pure conjugal union; and should exert every faculty to win the heart and hand of the one beloved; nor allow any thing to alienate their affections, because certain ruin to mind and body is consequent thereon.

VERY LARGE.—Possesses the element of conjugal union, and flowing together of soul, in the highest degree, and, with Continuity large, becomes broken-hearted when disappointed, and comparatively worthless in this world; seeks death rather than life; regards this union as the gem of life, and its loss as worse than death; and should manifest the utmost care to bestow itself only where it can be reciprocated for life.

FULL.—Can love cordially, yet is capable of changing its object, especially if Continuity be moderate; will love for life provided circumstances are favorable, yet will not bear every thing from a lover or companion, and, if one love is interrupted, will form another.

AVERAGE.—Is disposed to love but one for life, yet is capable of changing its object, and, with Secretiveness and Approbativeness large, and Conscientiousness only full, is capable of coquetry, especially if Amativeness is large, and Adhesiveness only full, and the temperament more powerful than fine-grained; such should cultivate this faculty, and not allow their other faculties to break their first love.

MODERATE.—Is somewhat disposed to love only once, yet allows other stronger faculties to interrupt first love, and, with Amativeness large, can form one attachment after another with comparative ease, yet is not true as a lover, nor faithful to first love.

SMALL.—Cares but little for first love, and seeks the promiscuous society and affection of the opposite sex, rather than a single partner for life.

VERY SMALL.—Manifests none of this faculty, and experiences too little to be cognizable.

4. INHABITIVENESS.

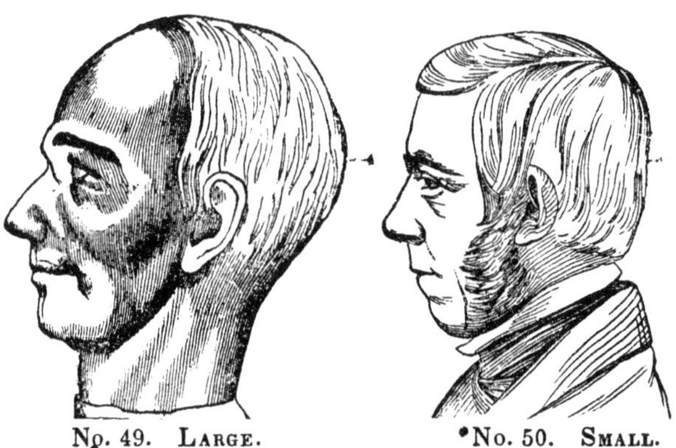

No. 49. LARGE. No. 50. SMALL.

The HOME feeling; love of HOUSE, the PLACE where one was born or has lived, and of home associations. Adapted to man's need of an abiding place, in which to exercise the family feelings; patriotism. Perversion—homesickness when away from home.

LARGE.—Has a strong desire to locate young, to have a home or room exclusively to itself; leaves home with great reluctance, and returns with extreme delight; soon becomes attached to house, sleeping-room, garden, fields, furniture, etc.; and highly prizes domestic associations; nor is satisfied till it has a place on which to expend this home instinct; with Philoprogenitiveness, Adhesiveness, Individuality, and Locality large, will love to travel, yet be too fond of home to stay away long at a time; may be a cosmopolite in early life, and see much of the world; but will afterward settle down in one spot; but with Approbativeness and Combativeness large, will defend national honor, praise its own country, government, etc.; and defend both country and fireside with great spirit; with Ideality large, is well adapted to beautify home; with Friendship large, will delight to see friends at home, rather than abroad; with Alimentiveness large, will enjoy food at home better than elsewhere, etc.: p. 68.

VERY LARGE.—Is liable to be homesick when away from home, especially for the first time, and the more so if Philoprogenitiveness and Adhesiveness are large; will suffer almost any inconvenience, and foregr bright prospects rather than leave home; and remain in an inferior house or place of business, rather than change. Its combinations will be analogous to those under Inhabitiveness large: p. 68.

Full.—Prefers to live in one place, yet willingly changes it when interest or the other faculties require it; and with large Philoprogenitiveness, Adhesiveness, and Amativeness, will think more of family and friends than of the domicile: p. 69.

Average.—Loves home tolerably well, yet with no great fervor, and changes the place of abode as the other faculties may dictate; takes no great interest in house or place, as such, or pleasure in their improvement, and is satisfied with ordinary home comforts; with Acquisitiveness large, spends reluctantly for its improvement; with Constructiveness moderate, takes little pleasure in building additions to home; with Individuality and Locality large, loves traveling more than staying in one place, and is satisfied with inferior home accommodations: p. 68.

Moderate or Small.—Cares little for home; leaves it without much regret; contemplates it with little delight; takes little pains in its improvement; and with Acquisitiveness large, spends reluctantly for its improvement: p. 69.

Very Small.—Experiences almost none of this faculty, and manifests still less: p. 69.

---

6. CONTINUITY.

No. 51. Large. No 52. Small.

A patient dwelling upon one thing till it is finished; consecutiveness and connectedness of thought and feeling.

Adapted to man's need of doing one thing at a time. Perversion—prolixity, repetition, and excessive amplification.

Large.—Gives the whole mind to the one thing in hand till it is finished; completes as it goes; keeps up one common train of thought, or current of feeling, for a long time; is disconcerted if attention is directed to a second object, and cannot duly consider another; with Adhesiveness large, pores sadly over the loss of friends for months and years; with the Moral faculties large, is uniform and consistent in religious exercises and character; with Combativeness and Destructiveness large, retains grudges and dislikes for a long time; with Ideality, Comparison, and Language large, amplifies figures of speech, and sustains figurative expressions; with the intellectual faculties strong, cons and pores over one thing, and imparts a unity and completeness to intellectual investigations; becomes thorough in whatever study it commences, and delays rather than commences mental operations: p. 70.

Very Large.—Fixes the mind upon objects slowly, yet cannot leave them unfinished; has great application, yet lacks intensity or point; is tedious, prolix, and thorough in few things, rather than an amateur in many: p. 70.

Full.—Dwells continuously upon subjects, unless especially called to others; prefers to finish up the matter in hand, and can, though with difficulty, give attention to other things; with the business organs large, makes final settlements; with the feelings large, fixes their action, yet is not monotonous, etc.: p. 71.

Average.—Can dwell upon things, or divert attention to others, as occasion requires; is not confused by interruption, yet prefers one thing at a time; with the intellectual organs large, is not a smatterer, nor yet profound; with the mental temperament, is clear in style, and consecutive in idea, yet never tedious; with Comparison large, manufactures expressions and ideas consecutively, and connectedly, and always to the point, yet never dwells unduly: p. 70.

Moderate.—Loves and indulges variety, and change of thought, feeling, occupation, etc.; is not confused by them; rather lacks application; with a good intellectual lobe, and an active temperament, knows a little about a good many things, rather than much about any one thing; with an active organization thinks clearly, and has unity and intensity of thought and feeling, yet lacks connectedness; with large Language and small Secretiveness, talks easily, but not long at a time upon one thing; does better on the spur of the moment, than by previous preparation; and should cultivate consistency of character and fixedness of mind, by finishing as he goes all he begins: p. 71.

Small.—With activity great, commences many things, yet finishes few; craves novelty and variety; puts many irons into the fire; lacks application; jumps rapidly from premise to conclusion, and fails to connect and carry out ideas; is a creature of impulse; lacks steadiness and consistency of character; may be brilliant, yet cannot be profound; humming-bird like, flies rapidly from thing to thing, but does not stay long; has many good thoughts, yet they are scattered; and talks on a great variety of subjects in a short time, but fails sadly in consecutiveness of feeling, thought, and action. An illustrative anecdote. An old and faithful servant to a passionate, petulant master, finally told him he could endure his testiness no longer, and must leave, though with extreme reluctance. "But," replied the master, "you know I am no sooner mad than pleased again." "Aye, but," replied the servant, "you are no sooner pleased than mad again:" p. 71.

VERY SMALL.—Is restless, and given to perpetual change; with activity great, is composed of gusts and counter-gusts of passion, and never one thing more than an instant at a time: p. 72.

SELFISH PROPENSITIES.

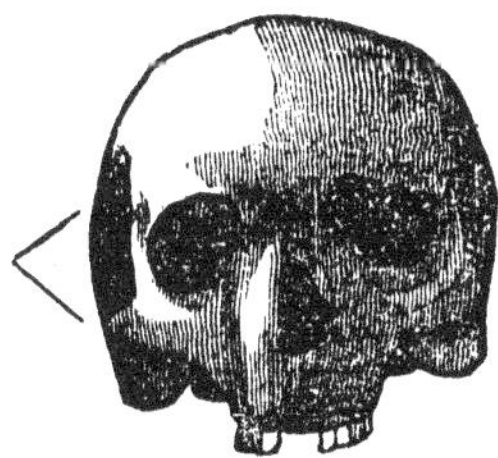

No. 53. LARGE.

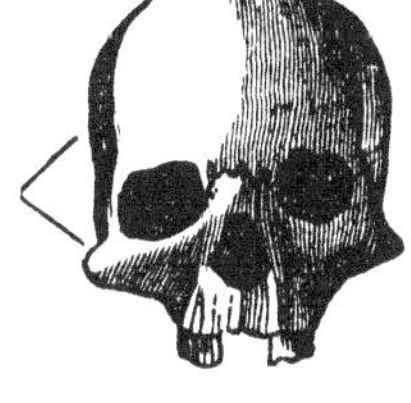

No. 54. SMALL.

These provide for man's ANIMAL wants; create those desires and instincts which relate more especially to his animal existence and habitual wants.

LARGE.—Gives strong animal desires; creates that selfishness which takes good care of number one; is strongly attached to this world and its pleasures; and, with activity great, uses vigorous exertions to accomplish worldly and personal ends; with the moral organs less than the selfish, connected with bodily disease, is liable to the depraved and sen sual manifestation; but with the moral and intellectual organs large, and a healthy organization, gives force, energy, determination, and that efficiency which accomplishes much.

VERY LARGE.—Experiences these animal impulses with still greater intensity; enjoys animal existence and pleasures with the keenest relish; and with great excitability or a fevered state of body, produces a strong tendency to sensual gratification, and sinful desires; yet when properly directed, and sanctified by the higher faculties, gives tremendous force of character, and energy of mind.

FULL.—Creates a good share of energy and physical force, yet no more than is necessary to cope with surrounding difficulties; and, with large moral and intellectual faculties, manifests more mental than physical force.

AVERAGE.—Gives a fair share of animal force, yet hardly enough to grapple with life's troubles and wrongs; with large moral and intellectual faculties, has more goodness than efficiency, and enjoys quiet more than conflict with men; and fails to manifest what goodness and talent are possessed.

MODERATE.—Rather lacks efficiency; yields to difficulties; wants fortitude and determination; fails to assert and maintain rights; and with large moral organs, is good-hearted, moral, etc.; yet borders on tameness.

SMALL, OR VERY SMALL.—Accomplishes little; lacks courage and force, and with large intellectual organs, is talented, yet utterly fails to manifest that talent; and with large moral organs, is so good as to be good for nothing.

E. VITATIVENESS.

TENACITY of life; resistance to death; love of existence as such; dreads annihilation; loves life, and clings tenaciously to it for its own sake.

LARGE.—Struggles resolutely through fits of sickness, and will not give up to die till it is absolutely compelled to do so. With large animal organs, clings to life on account of this world's gratifications; with large moral organs, to do good—to promote human happiness, etc.; with large social faculties, loves life both for its own sake and to bless family; with very large Cautiousness, dreads to change the present mode of existence, and with large and perverted Veneration and Conscientiousness, and small Hope, has an indescribable dread of entering upon an untried future state; but with Hope large, and a cultivated intellect, expects to exist hereafter, etc.

Very Large.—Shrinks from death, and clings to life with desperation; struggles with the utmost determination against disease and death; nor gives up to die till the very last, and then by the hardest; with Cautiousness very large, and Hope moderate, shudders at the very thought of dying, or being dead; but with Hope large, expects to live against hope and experience. Combinations like those under large, allowance being made for the increase of this faculty.

Full.—Loves life, and clings tenaciously to it, yet not extravagantly; hates to die, yet yields to disease and death, though reluctantly.

Average.—Enjoys life, and clings to it with a fair degree of earnestness, yet by no means with passionate fondness; and with a given constitution and health, will die easier and sooner than with this faculty large.

Moderate or Small.—Likes to live, yet cares no great about existence for its own sake; with large animal or domestic organs, may wish to live on account of family, or business, or worldly pleasure, yet cares less about it for its *own sake*, and yields up existence with little reluctance or dread.

Very Small.—Has no desire to live merely for the sake of living, but only to gratify other faculties.

---

6. COMBATIVENESS.

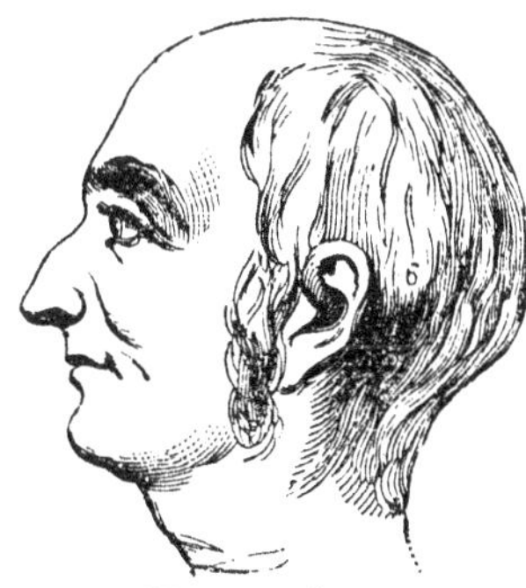

No. 55. Large.

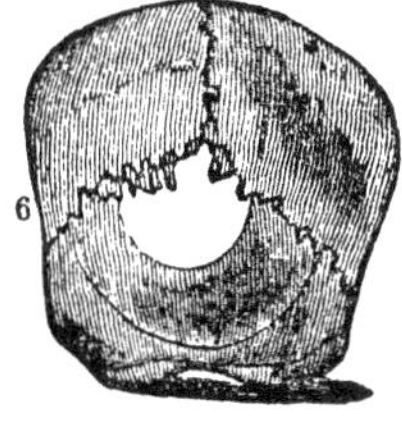

No. 56. Small.

Resistance; opposition; defence; defiance; boldness; courage; resentment; spirit; willingness to encounter;

SELF-PROTECTION; PRESENCE OF MIND; DETERMINATION; GET-OUT-OF-MY-WAY; LET-ME-AND-MINE-ALONE. Adapted to man's requisition for overcoming obstacles, contending for rights, etc. Perversion—anger; contrariety; fault-finding; contention; ill-nature; and fighting.

LARGE.—Imparts a bold, resolute, fearless, determined spirit; disposes to grapple with and remove obstacles, and drives whatever it undertakes; loves debate and opposition; gives great coolness, intrepidity, and presence of mind in time of danger, and nerves one for encounter; with large Philoprogenitiveness, takes the part of children; with large Inhabitiveness, defends country; with a powerful muscular system, enhances the strength in lifting, working, and all kinds of manual labor; with great Vitativeness and Destructiveness, defends life with desperation; with large Acquisitiveness maintains pecuniary rights, and drives money-making plans; with large Approbativeness, resents insult, and large Adhesiveness added, defends the character of friends; with full or large Self-Esteem, defends personal interest, takes its own part with spirit, and repels all aggressions; with Self-Esteem small, and Benevolence and Friendship large, defends the interest of friends more than of self; with large Conscientiousness, prosecutes the right, and opposes the wrong; with large intellectual organs, imparts vigor, power, and impressiveness to thoughts, expressions, etc.; with disordered nerves, is peevish, fretful, fault-finding, irritable, dissatisfied, unreasonable, and fiery in anger, and should first restore the nerves to health, and then restrain this fault-finding disposition, by remembering that the cause is IN THEM, instead of in what they fret at: p. 75.

VERY LARGE manifests those functions ascribed to Combativeness large, only in a still higher degree; and with a fevered stomach, is afflicted and torments others with an ungovernable temper, together with unqualified bitterness and hatefulness: p. 77.

FULL.—Evinces those feelings described under large, yet in a less degree, and is modified more by the larger organs; thus, with large moral and intellectual faculties, evinces much more moral than physical courage maintains the right and opposes the wrong—yet, with Firmness large, in a decided rather than in a combative spirit, etc.: p. 78.

AVERAGE.—Evinces the combative spirit according to circumstances: when vigorously opposed, or when any of the other faculties work in conjunction with Combativeness, shows a good degree of the opposing, energetic spirit; but, when any of the other faculties, such as large Cautiousness or Approbativeness work against it, it evinces irresolution, and even cowardice; with an active temperament, and disordered nerves, especially if dyspeptic, has a quick, sharp, fiery temper, yet lacks power of anger—will fret and threaten, yet will mean but little; with a large brain, and large moral and intellectual organs, will evince some intellectual and moral force, when once thoroughly roused, which will be but seldom; with large Approbativeness, and small Acquisitiveness, will defend character, but not pecuniary rights; with large Cautiousness, may be courageous where there is no danger, yet will run rather than fight; with smaller Cautiousness, will show some resentment when imposed upon, but submit rather tamely to injuries; with very large Philoprogenitiveness, and only average friendship, will resent any injuries offered to children with great spirit, yet not resent indignities offered to friends, etc.: p. 75.

MODERATE.—Rather lacks efficiency; with only fair muscles, is a poor worker, and fails to put forth even what little strength is possessed; with good moral and intellectual organs, possesses talent and moral worth, yet is easily overcome by opposition or difficulty; should seek some quiet occupation, where business comes in of itself, because it cannot urge itself unbidden upon the attention of others; is too good to be energetic; with weak Acquisitiveness, allows virtual robbery without resentment; with large Cautiousness, is tame and pusillanimous; with large Approbativeness, cannot stand rebuke, but will endure it; with moderate Self-Esteem and Hope, is all "I can't, it's hard," etc., and will not do well in life: p. 78.

SMALL.—Is inefficient; can accomplish little; never feels its own strength; and with large moral and intellectual organs, is too gentle and easily satisfied; with large Cautiousness, runs to others for protection, and is always complaining of its bad treatment: p. 79.

VERY SMALL.—Possesses scarcely any energy, and manifests none: p 79.

---

7. DESTRUCTIVENESS.

EXECUTIVENESS; SEVERITY; STERNNESS; the DESTROYING and PAIN-causing faculty; HARSHNESS; EXTERMINATION; INDIGNATION; disposition to BREAK, CRUSH, and TEAR DOWN; THE WALK-RIGHT-THROUGH-SPIRIT; adapted to man's destroying whatever is prejudicial to his happiness; performing and enduring surgical operations; undergoing pain, etc. Perversion—wrath; revenge; malice; disposition to murder, etc.

LARGE.—Imparts that determination, energy, and force which removes or destroys whatever impedes its progression; with Firmness large, gives that iron will which adheres till the very last, in spite of every thing, and carries its points any how; with large Combativeness, imparts a harsh rough mode of expression and action, and a severity, if not fierceness, to all its encounters; with large Acquisitiveness and Conscientiousness, will have every cent due, though it costs two to get it, yet wants no more, and retains grudges against those who have injured its pockets; with large Approbativeness and Combativeness, experiences determination and hostility toward those who trifle with reputation or impeach character; with large Self-Esteem, upon those who conflict with its interests, or detract from its supposed merits; with large Adhesiveness, when angry with friends, is very angry; with large Benevolence and Conscientiousness, employs a harsh mode of showing kindness; with large Comparison and Language, bestows very severe and galling epithets upon those who rouse it; with large Ideality, polishes and refines its expression of anger, and puts a keen edge upon its sarcasms, yet they are none the less cutting or efficient, etc. Such should avoid and turn from whatever provokes it: p. 82.

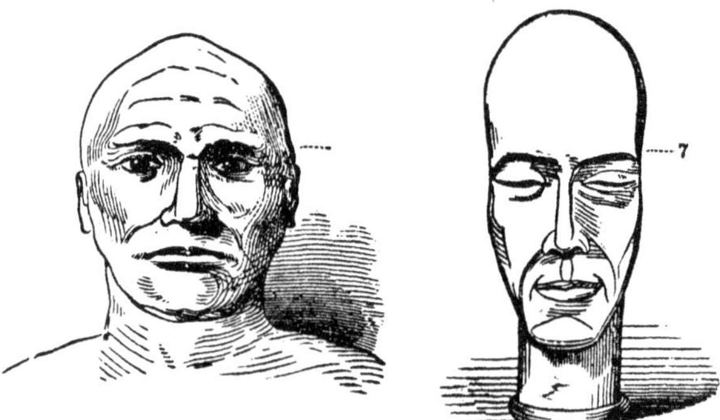

No. 57. LARGE. No. 58. SMALL.

VERY LARGE.—Feels the most powerful indignation, amounting even to rage and violence, when thoroughly provoked; and with large or very large Combativeness, acts like a chafed lion, and feels like rushing into the midst of perilous dangers. Such persons should never strike, for they will strike harder than they mean to, because it nerves the arm with unwonted strength. This faculty tears up and destroys whatever is in its way; is harsh and often morose in manner, and should cultivate pleasantness; with large Combativeness, Firmness, Self-Esteem, and Approbativeness moderate, is exceedingly repulsive, hating and hateful when angry, and is much more provoked than occasion requires; with large intellectuals, puts forth tremendous mental energy; and should offset this faculty by reason and moral feeling, and cultivate blandness instead of wrath: p. 83.

FULL.—Evinces a fair degree of this faculty, yet its tone and direction depend upon the larger organs; with large propensities, manifests much animal force; with large moral organs, evinces moral determination and force; with large intellectual organs, possesses intellectual might and energy, and thus of its other combinations; but with smaller Combativeness, is peaceful until thoroughly roused, but then rather harsh and vindictive; in boys, attacks only those it knows it can conquer, yet is then harsh; with smaller Self-Esteem, exercises this faculty more in behalf of others than of itself; with large Cautiousness and moderate Combativeness, keeps out of danger, broils, etc., till literally compelled to engage in them, but then becomes desperate, etc.: p. 83.

AVERAGE.—Manifests itself in a similar manner as when full, due allowance being made for diminished power: p. 82.

MODERATE.—Evinces but little harshness or severity; with large Benevolence, is unable to witness suffering or death, much less to cause them; will possess but little force of mind, or executiveness of character, to drive through great obstacles; with large moral organs added, will be more beloved than feared, and manifest extreme sympathy, amounting sometimes even to weakness, and secure ends more by mild than severe measures; with moderate Combativeness and Self-Esteem, is irresolute, unable to stand its ground, or to take care of itself; flies to others for protection; can do little, and feels that it can do still less; fails to realize or put forth its strength; and with large Cautiousness added, sees a lion where there is none, and makes mountains of mole-hills; and with small Hope added is literally good for nothing; but with large Hope and Firmness, and full Self-Esteem and Combativeness, accomplishes considerable, yet in a quiet way, and by perseverance more than force, by siege rather than by storm, and with large intellectual and moral faculties added, will be a good, yet not a tame, citizen; exert a good influence, and that always healthful, and be missed more when dead than prized while living. Those combinations under this organ large, reversed, apply to it when moderate: p 84.

SMALL.—With large moral faculties, possesses too tender a soul to enjoy our world as it is, or to endure hardships or cruelties; can neither endure nor cause suffering, and show so little as to provoke a smile or ridicule, and should cultivate hardness and force: p. 82.

VERY SMALL.—Experiences little, and manifests none of this faculty.

---

8. ALIMENTIVENESS.

APPETITE; the FEEDING instinct; RELISH for food; HUNGER adapted to man's need of food, and creating a disposition to eat. Perverted, it produces gormandizing and gluttony, and ends in dyspepsia and all its evils.

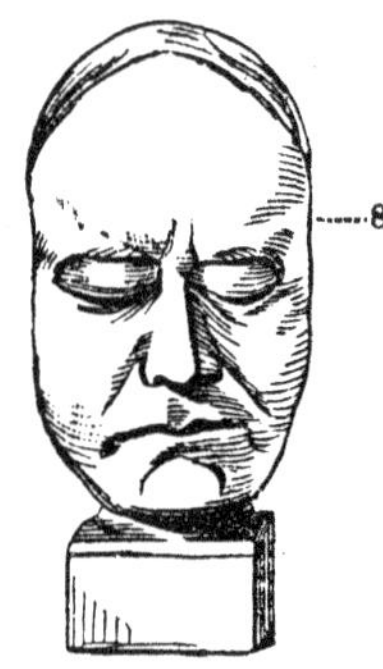

No. 59. LARGE. No. 60. SMALL.

LARGE.—Has a hearty relish for food; sets a high value upon table enjoyments, and solid, hearty food; with Acquisitiveness large, lays up abundance of food for future use—perhaps keeps so much on hand that some of it spoils; with Ideality large, must eat from a clean plate, and have food nicely cooked; with large Language and intellect, enjoys table-talk exceedingly, and participates in it; with large social faculties, must eat with others; is a good cook, if practiced in culinary arts; and with larger Approbativeness and Ideality than Causality, is apt to be ceremonious and over-polite at table, etc. Such should restrain this faculty by eating less, more slowly, and seldom: p. 86.

VERY LARGE.—Often eats more than is requisite; enjoys food exceedingly well; and hence is liable to clog body and mind by over-eating; should restrain appetite; will feel better by going without an occasional meal, and is liable to dyspepsia. This faculty is liable to take on a diseased action, and crave a much greater amount of food than nature requires, and hence is the great cause of dyspepsia. Its diseased action may be known by a craving, hankering, gone sensation before eating; by heart-burn, pain in the stomach, belching of wind, a dull, heavy, or painful sensation in the head, and a desire to be always nibbling at something; lives to eat, instead of eating to live, and should at once be erased by omitting one meal daily, and, in its stead, drinking abundantly of cold water. Abstemiousness will rectify this depraved appetite, while over-eating will only re-inflame both the stomach and its diseased hankering: p. 87.

FULL.—With a healthy stomach, eats freely what is offered, asking no questions; enjoying it, but not extravagantly; rarely over-eats, except when the stomach is disordered, and then experiences this hankering above described, which light eating alone can cure. For combinations, see Alimentiveness large: p. 87.

AVERAGE.—Enjoys food well, and eats with a fair relish; yet rarely over-eats except when rendered craving by dyspeptic complaints: p. 86.

MODERATE.—Rather lacks appetite; eats with little relish, and hence requires to pamper and cultivate appetite by dainties, and enjoying rich flavors; can relish food only when other circumstances are favorable; feels little hunger, and eats to live, instead of lives to eat; with Eventuality small, cannot remember from one meal to another what he had at the last: p. 87.

SMALL.—Eats with long teeth, and little relish; hardly knows or cares what or when he eats; and should pay more attention to duly feeding the body: p. 88.

VERY SMALL.—Is almost wholly destitute of appetite.

This faculty is more liable to perversion than any other, and excessive eating occasions more sickness, and depraves the animal faculties more than all other causes combined. Properly to feed the body, is of the utmost importance. Whenever this faculty becomes diseased, the first object should be to restore its natural function by abstinence. Medicines can never do it.

F. BIBATIVENESS OR AQUATIVENESS.

FONDNESS for LIQUIDS; desire to DRINK; love of WATER, washing, bathing, swimming, sailing, etc. Adapted to the existence and utility of water. Perversion—drinking in excessive quantities; drunkenness; and unquenchable thirst.

LARGE.—Loves to drink freely, and frequently; experiences much thirst; enjoys washing, swimming, bathing, etc., exceedingly, and is benefited by them; with Ideality large, loves water prospects.

VERY LARGE.—Is exceedingly fond of water, whether applied internally or externally; with large Adhesiveness and Approbativeness, and small Self-Esteem and Acquisitiveness, should avoid the social glass, lest he be overcome by it.

FULL.—Enjoys water well, but not extravagantly; drinks freely when the stomach is in a fevered state, and is benefited by its judicious external application.

AVERAGE.—Likes to drink at times, after working freely or perspiring copiously, yet cares no great about it.

MODERATE.—Partakes of little water, except occasionally, and is not particularly benefitted by its external application, further than is necessary for cleanliness; dislikes the shower or plunge baths, and rather dreads than enjoys sailing, swimming, etc., especially if Cautiousness is large.

SMALL.—Cares little for this element in any of its forms, or for any liquid food, and, with large Cautiousness, dreads to be on or near the water; with Alimentiveness large, prefers solid hard food to puddings or broth, etc.

VERY SMALL.—Has an unqualified aversion to water.

---

9. ACQUISITIVENESS.

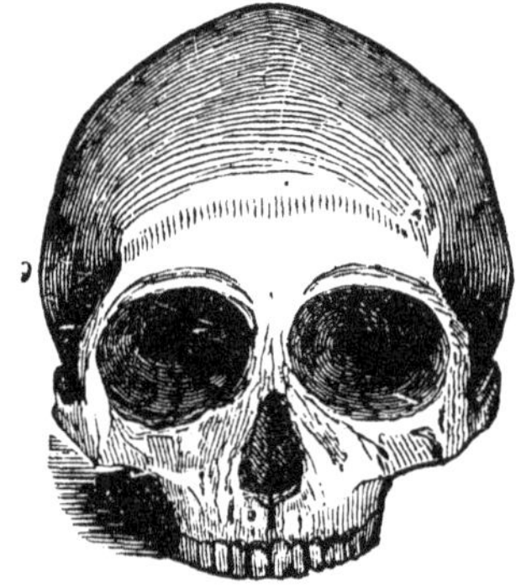

No. 61. LARGE

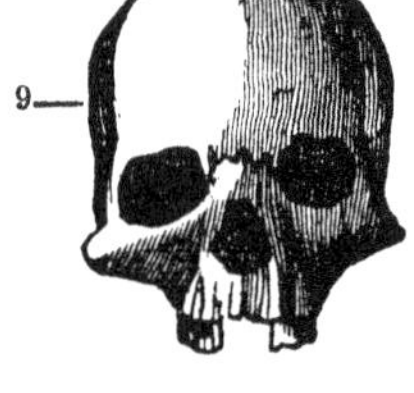

No. 62. SMALL.

ECONOMY; FRUGALITY; the ACQUIRING, SAVING, and HOARDING instinct; LAYING UP OF SURPLUS, and allowing nothing to be WASTED; desire to POSSESS and OWN; the MINE AND THINE FEELING; claiming of one's own things; love of TRADING AND AMASSING PROPERTY. Adapted to man's need of laying up the necessaries and comforts of life against a time of future need. Perversion—a miserly, grasping, close-fisted penuriousness.

LARGE.—Saves for future use what is not wanted for present; allows nothing to go to waste; turns every thing to a good account; buys closely, and makes the most of all it gets; is industrious, economical, and vigorously employs means to accumulate property and desires to own and possess much; with large social organs, industriously acquires property for domestic purposes, yet is saving in the family; with very large Adhesiveness and Benevolence, is industrious in acquiring property, yet spends it too freely upon friends; with large Hope added, is too apt to endorse for them; with small Secretiveness, and with activity greater than power, is liable to overdo, and takes so much work upon itself in order to save, as often to incur sickness, and thus loses more than gains; with large Approbativeness and small Secretiveness, tells how much property it possesses, but with large Secretiveness, keeps its own pecuniary affairs to itself; with large Constructiveness, inclines to make money by engaging in some mechanical branch of business: with large Cautiousness, is provident; with large Ideality, keeps its things very nice, and is tormented by whatever mars beauty; with large intellectual organs, loves to accumulate books, and whatever facilitates intellectual progress; with large Veneration and Self-Esteem, sets great store on antique and rare coins, and specimens, etc.: p. 89.

VERY LARGE.—Hastens to be rich; is too eager after wealth; too close in making bargains; too small and close in dealing; with large Cautiousness, is penny wise, but pound foolish; holds the sixpence too close to the eye to see the dollar further off, and gives its entire energies to amassing property; with smaller Secretiveness and large Conscientiousness, is close, yet honest, will have all its own, yet wants no more, and never employs deception; but, with large Secretiveness and but average Conscientiousness, makes money any how; palms off inferior articles for good ones, or at least over-praises what it wants to sell, and runs down what it buys; and with large Philoprogenitiveness and Perceptives added, can make a finished horse-jockey; with small Self-Esteem, is small and mean in deal, and sticks for the half cent; with very large Hope, and only full Cautiousness, embarks too deeply in business, and is liable to fail; with large Adhesiveness and Benevolence, will do for friends more than give, and circulate the subscription paper rather than sign it; with large Hope and Secretiveness, and only average Cautiousness, buys more than it can pay for, bases more in promises than in money, and should adopt a cash practice, and check the manifestations of this faculty by being less penurious and industrious, and more liberal: p. 92.

FULL.—Takes good care of what it possesses, and uses vigorous exertions to enhance them; values property for itself and its uses; is industrious, yet not grasping; and saving, without being close; with large Benevolence, is too ready to help friends; and with large Hope added, too liable to endorse; and with an active temperament, is too industrious to come to want; yet too generous ever to be rich. For additional combinations, see Acquisitiveness large: p. 93.

AVERAGE.—Loves property; yet the other faculties spend quite as fast as this faculty accumulates; with Cautiousness large or very large, loves property in order to be safe against future want; with large Approbativeness, desires it to keep up appearances; with large Conscientiousness to pay debts when it has the means; with large intellectual organs, will contribute to intellectual attainments; yet the kind of property and objects sought in its acquisition, depend upon other and larger faculties: p. 89.

MODERATE.—Values and makes property more for its uses than itself; seeks it as a means rather than an end; with Cautiousness large, may evince economy from fear of coming to want; or with other large organs, to secure other ends; yet cares no great for property on its own account; is rather wasteful; does not excel in bargaining, or like it; has no great natural pecuniary tact, or money-making capability, and is in danger of living quite up to income; with Ideality large, must have nice things, no matter if they are costly, yet does not take first-rate care of them; disregards small expenses; purchases to consume as soon as to keep; prefers to enjoy earnings now to laying them up; with large domestic organs, spends freely for family; with strong Approbativeness and moderate Cautiousness, is liable to be a spendthrift, and contract debts to make a display; with Hope large, runs deeply in debt, and spends money before it is earned; and thus of the other combinations: p. 94.

SMALL.—Holds money loosely; spends it often without getting its full value; cares little how his money goes; with Hope very large, enjoys his money to-day without saving for to-morrow; and with large Approbativeness and Ideality added, and only average Causality, is prodigal, and spends money to poor advantage; contracts debts without providing for their payment, etc. For additional combinations, see Acquisitiveness moderate: p. 95.

VERY SMALL.—Neither heeds nor knows the value of money; is wasteful; spends all it can get; lacks industry, and will be always in want: p. 95.

The back part of this organ, called Acquisition, accumulates property; the fore part, called Accumulation, saves; the former large and latter small, encompasses sea and land to make a dollar, and then throws it away, which is an American characteristic; and gets many things, but allows them to go to waste. Properly to spend money, implies a high order of wisdom. Every dollar should be made an instrument of the highest happiness.

10. SECRETIVENESS

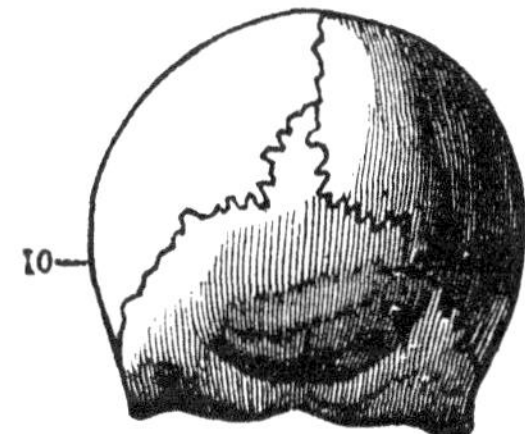

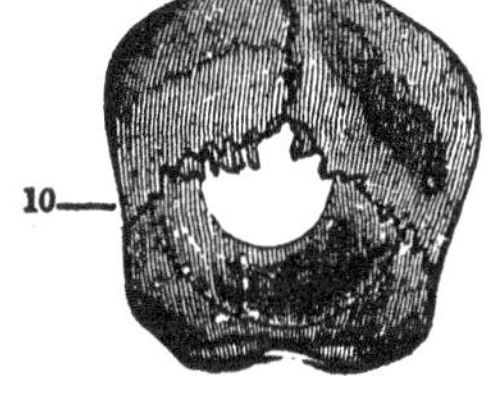

No. 63. LARGE. No. 64. SMALL.

SELF-GOVERNMENT; ability to RESTRAIN feelings; POLICY; MANAGEMENT; RESERVE; EVASION; DISCRETION; CUNNING; Adapted to man's requisition for controlling his animal nature. Perverted, it causes duplicity, double-dealing, lying, deception, and all kinds of false pretensions.

LARGE.—Throws a veil over the countenance, expression, and conduct; appears to aim at one thing while accomplishing another; loves to surprise others; is enigmatical, mysterious, guarded, foxy, politic, shrewd, managing, employs humbug, and is hard to be found out; with Cautiousness large, takes extra pains to escape detection; with Conscientiousness also large, will not tell a lie, yet will not always tell the truth; evades the direct question, and is equivocal in character; and though honest in purpose, yet resorts to many little cunning devices; with large intellectual organs and Cautiousness, expresses its ideas so guardedly as to lack distinctness and directness, and hence is often misunderstood; with large Approbativeness, takes many ways to secure notoriety, and hoists some false colors; with large Acquisitiveness, employs too much cunning in pecuniary transactions, and unless checked by still larger Conscientiousness, is not always strictly truthful or honest; with large social organs, forms few friendships, and those only after years of acquaintance, nor evinces half the attachment felt; is distant in society, and communicates, even with friends, only by piecemeal; divulges very few plans or business matters to acquaintances, or even to friends; lacks communicativeness, and has little or no fresh-hearted expression of feeling, but leaves an impression of uncertainty as to what they are and mean: p. 96.

VERY LARGE.—Is non-committal; cunning in the extreme with only average Conscientiousness, is deceptive, tricky, double-dealing, and unworthy to be trusted; with large Acquisitiveness added, will cheat as well as lie; with large Cautiousness, is unfathomable even by acknowledged friends; with very large Conscientiousness and large moral organs, and only average or full propensities, is not dangerous, and has a good moral basis, yet instinctively employs many stratagems, calculated to cast off suspicions on its motives; and should cultivate openness and sincerity: p. 98.

FULL.—Evinces much self-government; yet, if temperament be active, when the feelings do break forth, manifest themselves with unusual intensity; with large Acquisitiveness and Cautiousness, communicates but little respecting pecuniary affairs; with large Approbativeness, takes the popular side of subjects, and sails only with the current of public opinion; with Conscientiousness large, is upright in motive, and tells the truth, but not always the whole truth; and, though it hoists no false colors, it does not always show its own. For additional combinations, see Secretiveness large: p. 99.

AVERAGE.—Maintains a good share of self-government, except when under excitement, and then lets the whole mind out fully; with large Combativeness and an active temperament, though generally able to control resentment, yet, when once provoked, shows the full extent of its resentment; with large Cautiousness, sees that there is no danger before it lets the feelings fly; but with an excitable temperament, and especially a deranged stomach, shows a general want of policy and self-government, because the feelings are too strong to be kept in check; but if this faculty is manifested in connection with larger faculties, it evinces considerable power, yet is wanting when placed in opposition to them: p. 96.

MODERATE.—Expresses feelings with considerable fullness; pursues an open, direct course; is sincere and true; employs but little policy, and generally gives vent to thoughts and feelings; with Cautiousness large, evinces prudence in deeds, but imprudence in words; expresses opinions imprudently, yet is safe and circumspect in conduct; with large Acquisitiveness and Conscientiousness, prefers the one-price system in dealing, and cannot bear to banter; with large Adhesiveness, is a sincere, openhearted friend, and communicates with perfect freedom; with large Conscientiousness, and Combativeness added, is truthful, and speaks its whole mind too bluntly; with fine feelings, and a good moral organization, manifests the higher, finer feelings, without restraint or reserve, so as to be the more attractive; is full of goodness, and shows all that goodness without any intervening veil; manifests in looks and actions what is passing within; expresses all its mental operations with fullness, freedom, and force; chooses direct and unequivocal modes of expression; discloses faults as freely as virtues, and leaves none at a loss as to the real character; but with the harsher elements predominant, appears more hating and hateful than it really is; because it blows all its dislikes right out: p 100.

SMALL.—Is perfectly transparent; seems to be just what, and all that, it really is; disdains concealment in all its forms; is no hypocrite, but passive and unequivocal in all it says or does; carries the soul in the hands and face, and makes its way directly to the feelings, because it expresses itself so unequivocally; with large Cautiousness, is guarded in action, but unguarded in expression; frees its mind regardless of consequences, yet shows much prudence in other respects; with Conscientiousness large, loves the truth wherever it exists, and opens its mind freely to evidence and conviction; is open and above board in every thing, and allows all the mental operations to come right out, unveiled and unrestrained, so that their full force is seen and felt: p. 101.

VERY SMALL.—Conceals nothing, but discloses every thing: 101.

---

11. CAUTIOUSNESS.

No. 65. LARGE. No. 66. SMALL.

CAREFULNESS; WATCHFULNESS; PRUDENCE; PROVISION against want and danger; SOLICITUDE; ANXIETY; APPREHENSION; SECURITY; PROTECTION; AVOIDING prospective evils; the sentinel. Adapted to those dangers which surround us, and those provisions necessary for our future happiness. Perversion—irresolution; timidity; procrastination; indecision.

LARGE.—Is always on the look-out; takes ample time to get ready, provides against prospective dangers; makes every thing safe; guards against losses and evils; incurs no risk; sure binds that it may sure find; with large Combativeness, Hope, and an active temperament, drives, Jehu-like, whatever is undertaken, yet drives cautiously; lays on the the lash, yet holds a tight rein, so as not to upset its plans; with large Approbativeness, is doubly cautious as to character; with large Approbativeness and small Acquisitiveness, is extra careful of character, but not of money; with large Acquisitiveness and small Approbativeness takes special care of all money matters, but not of reputation; with large Adhesiveness and Benevolence, experiences the greatest solicitude for the welfare of friends; with large Conscientiousness, is careful to do nothing wrong; with large Causality, lays safe plans, and is judicious; with large Combativeness and Hope, combines judgment with energy and enterprise, and often seems reckless, yet is prudent; with large intellectual organs and Firmness, is cautious in coming to conclusions, and canvasses well all sides of the question, yet, once settled, is unmoved; with small Self-Esteem, relies too much upon the judgment of others, and too little upon itself; with large Philoprogenitiveness and disordered nerves, experiences unnecessary solicitude for children, and takes extra care of them, etc.: p. 104.

VERY LARGE.—With an excitable nervous system, procrastinates, puts off till to-morrow what ought to be done to-day; lacks promptness and decision, and refuses to run any risk; with only average or full Combativeness, Self-Esteem, and Hope, and large Approbativeness, accomplishes literally nothing, but should always act under others; with large Acquisitiveness, prefers small but sure gains to large but more risky ones, and safe investments to active business. For additional combinations, see Combativeness large, etc.: p. 105.

FULL.—Shows a good share of prudence and carefulness, except when the other faculties are powerfully excited; with large Combativeness and very large Hope, has but little prudence for his energy; is tolerably safe except when under considerable excitement; with large Acquisitiveness, is very careful whenever money or property are concerned; yet with only average Causality, evinces but little general prudence, and lays plans for the present rather than future, etc.: p. 105.

AVERAGE.—Has a good share of prudence, whenever this faculty works in connection with the larger organs, yet evinces but little in the direction of the smaller organs; with large Combativeness and Hope, and an excitable temperament, is practically imprudent, yet somewhat less so than appearances indicate; with large Causality, and only average Hope and Combativeness, and a temperament more strong than excitable, evinces good general judgment, and meets with but few accidents; but with an excitable temperament, large Combativeness and Hope, and only average or full Causality, will always be in hot water, fail to mature his plans, begin before he is ready, and be luckless and unfortunate in every thing, etc.: p. 103.

MODERATE.—With excitability great, acts upon the spur of the moment, without due deliberation; meets with many accidents caused by imprudence; with large Combativeness, is often at variance with neighbors with large Approbativeness, seeks praise, yet often incurs criticism; with average Causality and large Hope, is always doing imprudent things, and requires a guardian; with small Acquisitiveness keeps money loosely, and is easily over-persuaded to buy more than can be paid for; with large Philoprogenitiveness, loves to play with children, yet often hurts them; with large Language and small Secretiveness, says many very imprudent things, etc., and has a hard row to hoe; and with large Combativeness, has many enemies, but few friends, etc.: p. 106.

SMALL.—Is rash, reckless, luckless; and with large Hope, always in trouble; with large Combativeness, plunges headlong into difficulties in full sight, and should assiduously cultivate this faculty: p. 106.

VERY SMALL.—Has so little of this faculty, that its influence upon conduct is rarely ever perceived: p. 107.

---

12. APPROBATIVENESS.

DESIRE to be ESTEEMED; regard for CHARACTER, APPEARANCES, etc.; love of PRAISE; desire to EXCEL; AMBITION; AFFABILITY; POLITENESS; desire to DISPLAY and show off; sense of HONOR; desire for a GOOD NAME, for NOTORIETY, FAME, EMINENCE, DISTINCTION, and to be THOUGHT WELL OF; PRIDE of character; SENSITIVENESS to the speeches of people; and love of POPULARITY. Adapted to the reputable and disgraceful. Perversion—vanity; affectation; ceremoniousness; aristocracy; pomposity; eagerness for popularity; outside display, etc.

LARGE.—Loves commendation, and is cut by censure; is keenly alive to the smiles of public opinion; minds what people say; strives to show off to advantage, and is affable, courteous, and desirous of pleasing; loves to be in company; stands on etiquette and ceremony; aspires to do and become something great; sets much by appearances, and is mortified by reproach; with large Cautiousness and moderate Self-Esteem, is careful to take the popular side, and fears to face the ridicule of others; yet with

Conscience and Combativeness large, sticks to the right, though it is unpopular, knowing that it will ultimately confer honor; with large Benevolence, seeks praise for works of philanthropy and mercy; with large intellectual organs, loves literary and intellectual distinctions; with large Adhesiveness, desires the good opinion of friends, yet cares little for that of others; with large Self-Esteem, Combativeness, and excitability, is very touchy when criticised, seeks public life, wants all the praise, and hates rivals; with large perceptives, takes a forward part in literary and debating societies; with large Combativeness, Hope, and activity, will not be outdone, but rather work till completely exhausted, and liable to hurt itself by feats of rivalry: p. 108.

Very Large.—Sets every thing by the good opinion of others; is ostentatious, if not vain and ambitious; loves praise, and is mortified by censure inordinately; with moderate Self-Esteem and Firmness, cannot breast public opinion, but is over fond of popularity; with only average Conscience, seeks popularity without regard to true merit; but with large Conscience, seeks praise mainly for virtuous doings; with large Ideality, and only average Causality, seeks praise for fashionable dress and outside appearances rather than internal merit; and is both vain and fashionable as well as aristocratic, and starves the kitchen to stuff the parlor; with large Acquisitiveness, boasts of riches; with large Adhesiveness, boasts of friends; with large Language. is extra forward in conversation, and engrosses much of the time, etc. This is the main organ of aristocracy, exclusiveness, fashionableness, so-called pride, and nonsensical outside show: p. 110.

Full.—Values the estimation of others, yet will not go far out of the way to get it; seeks praise in connection with the larger organs, yet cares little for it in the direction of the smaller ones; is not aristocratic, yet likes to make a fair show in the world; with large Adhesiveness, loves the praise and cannot endure the censure of friends; with large Conscientiousness, sets much by MORAL character, and wishes to be praised for correct MOTIVES; yet, with moderate Acquisitiveness, cares little for the name of being rich; with large Benevolence and intellectual organs, desires to be esteemed for evincing talent in doing good, etc.: p. 110.

Average.—Evinces only a respectable share of this faculty, except when it is powerfully wrought upon by praise or reproach; is mortified by censure, yet not extremely so, and calls his other faculties to his justification; is not sufficiently ambitious to incur injury, yet is by no means deficient in this respect; and is not insensible to compliments, yet cannot well be inflated with praise: p. 107.

Moderate.—Feels some, but no great, regard for popularity; and evinces this faculty only in connection with the larger faculties; with large Self-Esteem and Firmness, is inflexible and austere; and with large

Combativeness and small Agreeableness, lacks civility and complaisance to others; disdains to flatter, and cannot be stuffed and should cultivate a pleasing, winning mode of address: p. 112.

SMALL.—Cares little for the opinions of others, even of friends; is comparatively insensible to praise; disregards style and fashion; despises etiquette and formal usages; never asks what will persons think, and puts on no outside appearances for their own sake; with large Self-Esteem, Firmness, and Combativeness, is destitute of politeness, devoid of ceremony, and not at all flexible or pleasing in manners; with large Combativeness and Conscientiousness, goes for the right regardless of popularity, and is always making enemies; says and does things in so graceless a manner as often to displease; with large Acquisitiveness and Self-Esteem, though wealthy, makes no boast of it, and is as commonplace in conduct as if poor, etc.: p. 112.

VERY SMALL.—Cares almost nothing for reputation, praise, or censure as such.

---

13. SELF-ESTEEM.

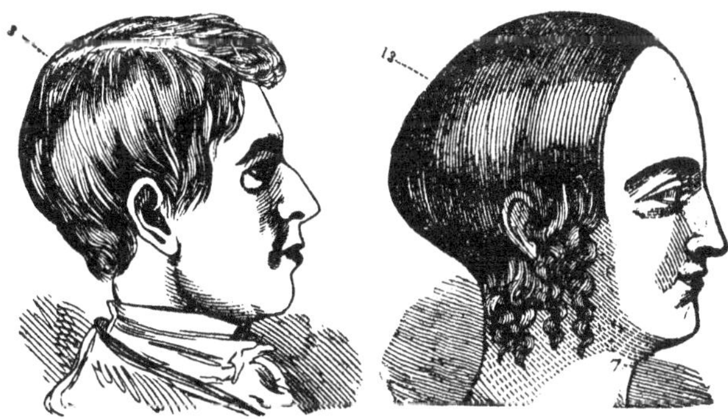

No. 67. LARGE. No. 68. SMALL.

SELF-appreciation and valuation; SELF-RESPECT and RELIANCE; MAGNANIMITY; NOBLENESS; INDEPENDENCE; DIGNITY; SELF-SATISFACTION and complacency; love of liberty and power; an ASPIRING, SELF-ELEVATING, RULING instinct; PRIDE of character; MANLINESS; LOFTY-MINDEDNESS, and desire for elevation. Adapted to the superiority, greatness, and exalted dignity of human nature. Perversion—haughtiness; forwardness; over-bearing; tyranny; egotism, and superciliousness.

LARGE.—Puts a high estimate upon itself, its sayings, doings, and capabilities; falls back upon its own unaided resources; will not take advice, but insists upon being its own master; is high-minded; will never stoop or demean itself; aims high; is not satisfied with moderate success, or a petty business, and comports and expresses itself with dignity, and perhaps with majesty, and is perfectly self-satisfied; with large Philoprogenitiveness, prides itself in its children, yet with Combativeness large, requires implicit obedience, and is liable to be stern; with large Adhesiveness, seeks society, yet must be its leader; with large Acquisitiveness added, seeks partnership, but must be the head of the firm; with large Firmness and Combativeness, cannot be driven, but insists upon doing its own will and pleasure, and is sometimes contrary and headstrong; with large Hope, thinks that any thing it does cannot possibly fail, because done so well; with large moral organs, imparts a tone, dignity, aspiration, and elevation of character, which commands universal respect; and with large intellectual faculties added, is desirous of, and well calculated for public life; is a natural leader, but seeks moral distinction, and leads the public mind; with large Combativeness, Destructiveness, Firmness, and Approbativeness, loves to be captain or general, and speaks with that sternness and authority which enforce obedience; with large Acquisitiveness aspires to be rich, the richest man in town, partly on account of the power wealth confers; with large Language, Individuality, Firmness, and Combativeness, seeks to be a political leader; with large Constructiveness, Perceptives, Causality, and Combativeness, is well calculated to have the direction of men, and oversee large mechanical establishments; with only average brain and intellect, and large selfish faculties, is proud, haughty, domineering, egotistical, overbearing, greedy of power and dominion, etc.: p. 114.

VERY LARGE.—Evinces the characteristics of large, only in a still higher degree; is very apt to be pompous, supercilious, proud, and imperious; will do nothing except it be on the largest scale; yet, unless Causality be large, is apt to fail, because ambition is too great for the calibre; with large Firmness, Approbativeness, and Hope, is a real aristocrat, and puts himself above every body else; with only average Approbativeness and Agreeableness, takes no pains to smooth off the rougher points of character, but is every way repulsive; with average Philoprogenitiveness, is very domineering in the family, and insists upon being waited upon, obeyed, etc; and should carry his head a little lower, and humble his proud soul: p. 116.

FULL.—Evinces a good degree of dignity and self-respect, yet is not proud or haughty; with large Combativeness, Firmness and Hope, relies fully upon its own energies in cases of emergency, yet is willing to hear advice though seldom takes it; conducts becomingly and secures respect; and with large Combativeness and Firmness, and full Destructiveness and Hope, evinces much power of this faculty, but little when these faculties are small: p. 116.

AVERAGE.—Shows this faculty mainly in combination with those that are larger; with large Approbativeness and Firmness, and a large brain and moral organs, rarely trifles or evinces meanness; yet is rarely conceited, and thinks neither too little nor too much of self, but places a just estimate upon its own capabilities; with large Adhesiveness, both receives and imparts character to friends, yet receives most; with large Conscientiousness, prides itself more on moral worth than physical qualities, wealth, titles, etc.; and with large intellectual and moral organs, values itself mainly for intellectual and moral excellence: p. 113.

MODERATE.—Rather underrates personal capabilities and worth; feels rather inferior, unworthy, and humble; lacks dignity and manliness, and is rather apt to say and do trifling things, and let itself down; with large intellectual and moral organs, leads off well when once placed in a responsible position, yet at first distrusts its own capabilities; with large Conscientiousness, Combativeness, and activity, often appears self-sufficient and positive, because certain of being right, yet it is founded more on reason than egotism; with large Approbativeness, loves to show off, and make others satisfied with its capabilities, yet is not satisfied with itself; goes abroad after praise, rather than feels internally conscious of its own merits; is apt to boast because it would make others appreciate its powers, while, if it were fully conscious of them, it would care less about the estimation of others; with large moral and intellectual powers, has exalted thoughts and aspirations, and communicates well, yet often detracts from them by commonplace phrases and undignified expressions; will be too familiar to be respected in proportion to merit, and should vigorously cultivate this faculty by banishing mean and cultivating high thoughts of self: p. 116.

SMALL.—Feels diminutive in its own eyes; lacks elevation and dignity of tone and manner; places a low estimate on self; and, with Approbativeness large, is more anxious to appear well in the eyes of others than in its own; with large Combativeness and Destructiveness, shows some self-reliance when provoked or placed in responsible positions, yet lacks that dignity and tone which commands universal respect, and gives a capability to lead off in society; lacks self-confidence and weight of character: shrinks from responsible and great undertakings, from a feeling of unworthiness; underrates itself, and is therefore undervalued by others, and feels insignificant as if in the way, or trespassing upon others, and hence often apologizes; and should feel constantly "I'm a man."

VERY SMALL.—Feels little, and manifests none of this faculty.

14. FIRMNESS.

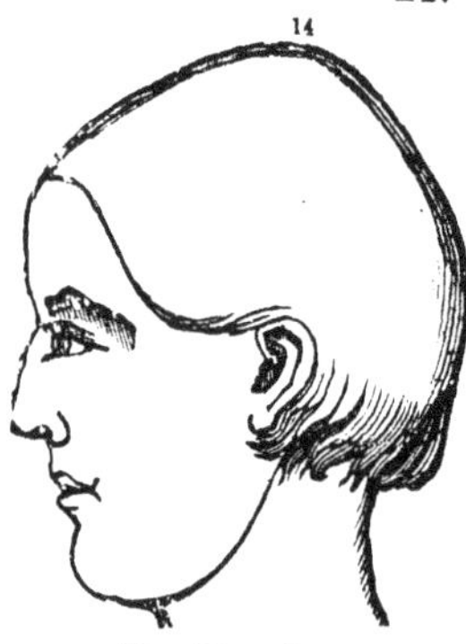

No. 69. LARGE.

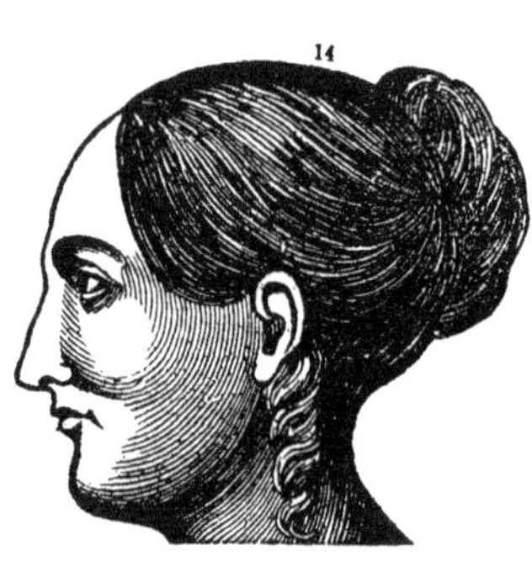

No. 70. SMALL.

STABILITY; DECISION; PERSEVERANCE; FIXEDNESS of purpose; TENACITY of WILL, and aversion to change. Adapted to man's requisition for holding out to the end. Perversion—obstinacy; wilfulness; mulishness; stubbornness; unwillingness to change, even though reason requires.

LARGE.—Is set in its own way; sticks to and carries out what it commences; holds on long and hard; continues to the end, and may be fully relied upon; with full Self-Esteem and large Combativeness, cannot be driven, but the more it is forced the more it resists; with large Combativeness and Destructiveness, adds perseverance to stability, and not only holds on, but drives forward determinedly through difficulties; with large Hope, undertakes much and carries it all out; with large Cautiousness and Causality, is careful and judicious in laying plans and forming opinions, yet rarely changes when once decided; may seem to waver until the mind is fully made up, but is afterward the more unchanging; with Hope very large, and Cautiousness and Causality only average, decides quickly, even rashly, and refuses to change; with Adhesiveness and Benevolence large, is easily persuaded, especially by friends, yet cannot be driven; and with large Cautiousness, Combativeness, Causality, perceptives, activity, and power, will generally succeed, because wise in planning and persevering in execution; with Combativeness and Self-Esteem large, and Causality only average, will not see the force of arguments against himself, but tenaciously adheres to affirmed opinions and purposes, yet is less firm than he seems to be; with large Conscientiousness and Combat tiveness, is doubly decided wherever right or justice are concerned, and in such cases will never give one inch, but will stand out in argument, effort, or as a juryman till the last: p. 119.

Very Large.—Is well-nigh obstinate, stubborn, and with large Combativeness and Self-Esteem, is unchangeable as the laws of the Medes and Persians, and can neither be persuaded nor driven; with large activity, power, brain, and intellectual organs, is well calculated to carry forward some great work which requires the utmost determination and energy; with large Causality, can possibly be turned by potent reasons, yet by nothing else: p. 120.

Full.—Like Firmness large, shows a great degree of decision, when this faculty works with large organs, but not otherwise; with Combativeness and Conscientiousness large, shows great Fixedness where right and truth are concerned, yet with Acquisitiveness moderate, lacks perseverance in money matters; with moderate Combativeness and Self-Esteem, is easily turned; and with large Adhesiveness and Benevolence, too easily persuaded, even against its better judgment; with Cautiousness and Approbativeness large, or very large, often evinces fickleness, irresolution, and procrastination; and with an uneven head, and an excitable temperament, often appears deficient in this faculty: p. 131.

Average.—When supported by large Combativeness, or Conscientiousness, or Causality, or Acquisitiveness, etc., shows a good degree of this faculty; but when opposed by large Cautiousness, Approbativeness, or Adhesiveness, evinces its deficiency, and has not enough of this faculty for great undertakings: p. 119.

Moderate.—Rather lacks perseverance, even when his larger faculties support it, and when they do not, evinces fickleness, irresolution, indecision, and lacks perseverance; with Adhesiveness large, is too easily persuaded and influenced by friends; with large Cautiousness and Approbativeness and moderate or small Self-Esteem, is flexible and fickle, and goes with the current: p. 132.

Small.—With activity great, and the head uneven, is fitful, impulsive, and, like the weather-vane, shifts with every changing breeze, and is ruled by the other faculties; and as unstable as water: p. 122

Very Small.—Is changed by the slightest motives; is a perfect creature of circumstances, and accomplishes nothing requiring perseverance: p. 122.

MORAL FACULTIES.

These render man a moral, accountable, and religious being, humanize, adorn, and elevate his nature; connect him with the moral nature of things; create his higher and nobler sentiments; beget aspirations after goodness, virtue, purity, and moral principle, and ally him to angels and to God.

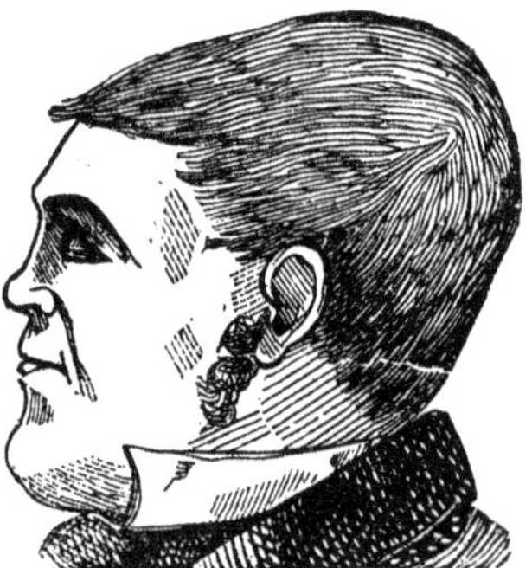

No. 71. LARGE. No. 72. SMALL.

LARGE.—Create a high regard for things sacred and religious; give an elevated, moral, and aspiring cast of feelings and conduct; create right intentions, and a desire to become good, holy, and moral in feeling and conduct; and, with weak animal feelings, is a rose in the shade.

VERY LARGE.—Give a most exalted sense and feeling of the moral and religious, with a high order of practical goodness, and the strongest aspirations for a higher and holier state, both in this life and that which is to come.

FULL.—Has a good moral and religious tone, and general correctness of motive, so as to render feelings and conduct about right; but with strong propensities and only average intellectual faculties, is sometimes led into errors of belief and practice; means right, yet sometimes does wrong, and should cultivate these faculties, and restrain the propensities.

AVERAGE.—Surrounded by good influences, will be tolerably moral and religious in feeling, yet not sufficiently so to withstand large propensities; with disordered nerves, is quite liable to say and do wrong things, yet afterward repents, and requires much moral cultivation.

MODERATE.—Has a rather weak moral tone; feels but little regard for things sacred and religious; is easily led into temptation; feels but little moral restraint; and, with large propensities, especially if circumstances favor their excitement, is exceedingly liable to say and do what is wrong.

SMALL.—Has weak moral feeling; lacks moral character; and, with large propensities, is liable to be depraved, and a bad member of society.

VERY SMALL.—Feels little, and shows no moral tone

15. CONSCIENTIOUSNESS.

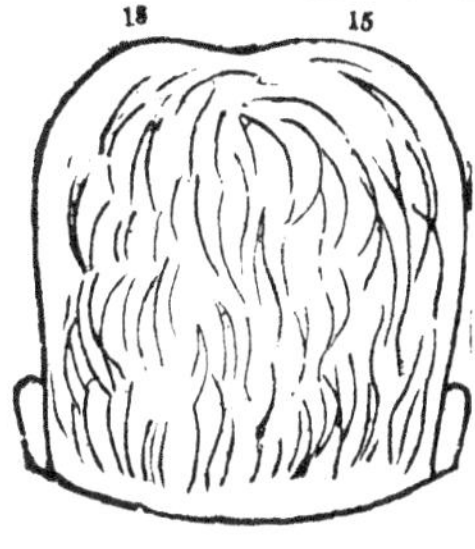

No. 73. Large.

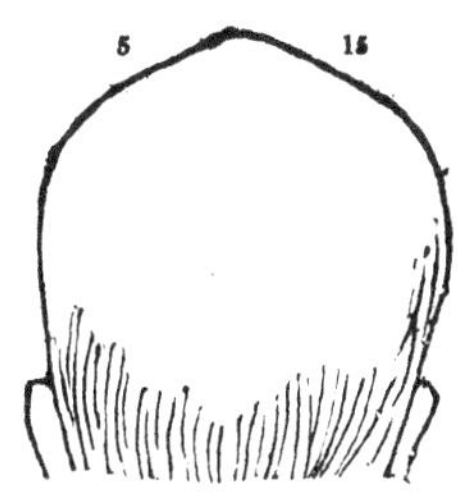

No. 74. Small.

Moral principle ; integrity ; perception and love of right ; innate sense of accountability and obligation ; love of justice and truth ; regard for duty ; desire for moral purity and excellence ; disposition to fulfill promises, agreements, etc. ; the internal monitor which approves the right and condemns the wrong ; sense of guilt ; contrition ; desire to reform ; penitence ; forgiveness. Adapted to the rightness of right, and the wrongness of wrong, and to the moral nature and constitution of things. Perverted, it makes one do wrong from conscientious scruples, and torments with undue self-condemnation.

Large.—Loves the right as right, and hates the wrong because wrong ; is honest, faithful, upright in motive ; means well ; consults duty before expediency ; feels guilty when conscious of having done wrong ; desires forgiveness for the past, and to do better in future ; with strong propensities, will sometimes do wrong, and then be exceedingly sorry therefor ; and, with a wrong education added, is liable to do wrong, thinking it to be right, because these propensities warp conscience, yet means right ; with large Cautiousness, is solicitous to know what is right, and careful to do it ; with weaker Cautiousness, sometimes does wrong carelessly or indifferently, yet afterward repents it ; with large Cautiousness and Destructiveness, is severe on wrong doers, and unrelenting until they evince penitence, and then cordially forgives ; with large Approbativeness, keeps the moral character pure and spotless—values others on their morals more than wealth, birth, etc., and makes his word his bond ; with large Benevolence, Combativeness, and Destructiveness, feels great indignation and severity against oppressors, and those who cause others sufferings by wronging them ; with large Ideality, has strong aspirations after moral purity and excellence ; with large reasoning faculties, takes great pleasure, and shows much talent in reasoning upon, and investigating moral subjects, etc. : p. 126.

VERY LARGE.—Places moral excellence at the head of all excellence, is governed by the highest order of moral principle; would on no account knowingly do wrong; is scrupulously exact in all matters of right; perfectly honest in motive; always condemning self and repenting; makes duty every thing; very forgiving of those who evince penitence, but inexorable without; with Combativeness large, evinces the utmost indignation at the wrong, and drives the right with great force; is censorious, and makes but little allowance for the faults and follies of mankind, and shows extraordinary moral courage and fortitude ; with small Secretiveness and an active temperament, is liable to denounce evil doers; with large Friendship, cannot tolerate the least thing wrong in friends, and is liable to reprove them ; with large Philoprogenitiveness, exacts too much from children, and with large Combativeness, is too liable to blame them; with large Cautiousness, is often afraid to do lest it should do wrong; with large Veneration, reasoning faculties, and Language, is a natural theologian, and takes the highest pleasure in reasoning and conversing upon all things having a moral and religious bearing; with Veneration average, and Benevolence large or very large, cannot well help being a thorough-going reformer, etc. : p. 129.

FULL.—Has good conscientious feelings, and correct general intentions, yet is not quite as correct in action as intentions; means well, yet with large Combativeness, Destructiveness, Amativeness, etc., may sometimes yield to these faculties, especially if the system is somewhat inflamed; with large Acquisitiveness, makes very close bargains, and will take such advantages as are common in business, yet does not intend to wrong others out of their just dues, still, has more regard for money than justice; with large intellectual organs, loves to reason upon subjects where right and duty are involved, yet too often takes the ground of expediency, and fails to allow right its due weight; and should never allow conscience to be in any way weakened, but should cultivate it assiduously: p. 130.

AVERAGE.—When not tempted by stronger faculties does what is about right; generally justifies itself, and does not feel particularly indignant at the wrong, or commendatory of the right; with large Approbativeness and Self-Esteem, may do an honorable thing, yet where honor and right clash, will choose the former; with only average Combativeness and Destructiveness, allows many things that are wrong to pass unrebuked, or even unresented, and shows no great moral indignation or force; with moderate or small Secretiveness and Acquisitiveness, and large Approbativeness Benevolence, and Ideality, will do as nearly right, and commit as few errors as those with Secretiveness, Acquisitiveness and Conscientiousness all large, and may be trusted, especially on honor, yet will rarely feel guilty, and should never be blamed, because Approbativeness will be mortified before conscience is convicted; with large propensities, especially Secretiveness and Acquisitiveness, and only full Benevolence, is selfish; should be dealt with cautiously, and thoroughly bound in writing, because liable to be slippery, tricky, etc.; and should cultivate this faculty by never allowing the propensities to overcome it, and by always considering things in the moral aspect: p. 124.

MODERATE.—Has some regard for duty in feeling, but less in practice; justifies self; is not very penitent or forgiving; even temporizes with principle, and sometimes lets interest rule duty. The combinations under average apply still more forcibly here: p. 131

SMALL.—Has few conscientious scruples; has little penitence, gratitude, or regard for moral principle, justice, duty, etc.; and is governed mainly by his larger faculties; with large propensities and only average Veneration and Spirituality, evinces a marked deficiency of moral principle; with moderate Secretiveness and Acquisitiveness, and only full Destructiveness and Combativeness, and large Adhesiveness, Approbativeness, Benevolence, Ideality, and intellect, and a fine temperament, may live a tolerably blameless life, yet, on close scrutiny, will lack the moral in feeling, but may be safely trusted because true to promises; that is, conscience having less to contend with, its deficiency is less observable. Such should most earnestly cultivate this faculty: p. 132.

VERY SMALL.—Is almost wholly destitute of moral feeling, and wholly controlled by the other faculties: p. 133.

---

16. HOPE.

EXPECTATION; ANTICIPATION of future success and happiness. Adapted to man's relations with the future. Perverted, it becomes visionary and castle-building.

LARGE.—Expects much from the future; contemplates with pleasure the bright features of life's picture; never desponds; overrates prospective good, and underrates and overlooks obstacles and evils; calculates on more than the nature of the case will warrant; expects, and hence attempts a great deal, and is therefore always full of business; is sanguine, and rises above present trouble by hoping for better in future, and though disappointed, hopes on still; builds some air castles, and lives in the future more than in the present; with large Combativeness, Firmness, and Causality, is enterprising, never gives up the ship, but struggles manfully through difficulties; and with large Approbativeness, and full Self-Esteem added, feels adequate to difficulties, and grapples with them spiritedly; with large Self-Esteem, thinks that every thing it attempts must succeed, and with large Causality added, considers its plans well-nigh perfect; with large Acquisitiveness lays out money freely in view of future gain; with large Approbativeness and Self-Esteem, hopes for renown, honor, etc.; with large Veneration and Spirituality, hopes to attain exalted moral excellence, and should check it by acting on only half it promises, and reasoning against it· p. 137.

VERY LARGE.—Has unbounded expectations; builds a world of castles in the air; lives in the future; enjoys things in anticipation more than in possession; with small Continuity, has too many irons in the fire; with an active temperament added, takes on more business than it can work off properly; is too much hurried to do things in season; with large Acquisitiveness, is grasping, counts chickens before they are hatched, and often two to the egg at that; with only average Cautiousness, is always in hot water; never stops to enjoy what it possesses, but grasps after more, and will never accomplish much because it undertakes too much, and in taking one step forward slips two steps back: p. 138.

FULL.—Expects considerable, yet realizes more; undertakes no more than it can accomplish; is quite sanguine and enterprising, yet with Cautiousness large, is always on the safe side; with large Acquisitiveness added, invests money freely, yet always safely, makes good bargains, if any, and counts all the cost, yet is not afraid of expenses where it knows they will more than pay; with larger animal faculties than moral, will hope more for this world's goods than for another, and with larger moral than animal, for another state of being than this, etc.: p. 139.

AVERAGE.—Expects and attempts too little, rather than too much; with large Cautiousness, dwells more on difficulties than encouragements; is contented with the present rather than lays out for the future; with large Acquisitiveness added, invests his money very safely, if at all, and prefers to put it out securely on interest rather than risk it in business, except in a perfectly sure business; will make money slowly, yet lose little, and with large intellectual organs, in the long run may acquire considerable wealth: p. 136.

MODERATE.—With large Cautiousness, makes few promises; but with large Conscientiousness, scrupulously fulfills them, because it promises only what it *knows* can be performed; with Small Self-Esteem, and large Veneration, Conscientiousness, and Cautiousness, if a professed Christian, will have many fears as to his future salvation; with only average propensities, will lack energy, enterprise, and fortitude; with large Firmness and Cautiousness, is very slow to embark, yet once committed.

rarely backs out; with large reasoning faculties, may be sure of success, because it sees *why and how* it is to be brought about; with large Acquisitiveness, will hold on to what money it gets, or at least spend very cautiously, and only where it is sure to be returned with interest; should cheer up, never despond, count favorable but not unfavorable chances, keep up a lively, buoyant state of mind, and "hope on, hope ever:" p. 139.

SMALL.—Expects and undertakes very little; with large Cautiousness, puts off till it is too late; is always behind; may embark in projects after every body else has succeeded, but will then be too late, and in general knocks at the door just after it has been bolted; with large Cautiousness, is forever in doubt; with large Approbativeness and Cautiousness, though most desirous of praise, has little hopes of obtaining it, and therefore is exceedingly backward in society, yet fears ridicule rather than hopes for praise; is easily discouraged; sees lions in the way; lacks enterprise; magnifies obstacles, etc.: p. 140.

VERY SMALL.—Expects next to nothing, and undertakes little: p. 140.

---

17. SPIRITUALITY.

FAITH; PRESCIENCE; the "LIGHT WITHIN;" TRUST in DIVINE GUIDING; perception and feeling of the SPIRITUAL; interior perception of TRUTH, what is BEST, what is about to transpire, etc. Adapted to a spiritual state of mind and feeling. Perversion—superstition; witchcraft; and with Cautiousness large, fear of ghosts.

LARGE.—Perceives and knows things independent of the senses or intellect, or as it were by spiritual intuition; experiences an internal consciousness of what is best, and that spiritual communion with God which constitutes the essence of true piety; loves to meditate; bestows a species of waking clairvoyance, and is as it were "forewarned of God;" combined with large Veneration, holds intimate communion with the Deity, for whom it experiences profound adoration; and takes a world of pleasure in that calm, happy, half-ecstatic state of mind caused by this faculty; with large Causality, perceives truth by intuition, which philosophical tests prove to be correct; with large Comparison added, has a deep and clear insight into spiritual subjects, and embodies a vast amount of the highest order of truth; with vigorous propensities, gives them a sanctified cast and spiritual direction; and clearly perceives, and fully realizes, a spiritual state of being after death: p. 142.

VERY LARGE.—Experiences the same functions as large, only in a higher degree; unless well regulated by reason, is liable to fanciful credulity, fanaticism, and superstition, and to a thousand whims, visions, dreams, etc.: p. 143.

FULL.—Has a full share of high, pure, and spiritual feeling; has many premonitions, or interior warnings and guidings, which, implicitly followed, would conduct to success and happiness through life; and has an inner test or touchstone of truth, right, etc., in a kind of inner consciousness which is independent of reason, yet, unperverted, in harmony with it; is quite spiritual-minded, and as it were "led by the spirit." For combinations, see large: p. 143.

AVERAGE.—Has some spiritual premonitions and guidings, yet they are not always sufficiently distinct to secure their being followed; but, when followed, they lead correctly; sees this light within, and feels what is true and best, with tolerable distinctness, and should cultivate this faculty by following its light: p. 141.

MODERATE.—Has some, but not very distinct perception of spiritual things; rather lacks faith; believes mainly from evidence and little from intuition; with large Causality, says "Prove it," and takes no man's say so unless he gives good *reasons:* p. 144.

SMALL.—Perceives spiritual truths so indistinctly as rarely to admit them; is not guided by faith, because so weak; like disbelieving Thomas, must see the fullest PROOF before it believes; has very little credulity, and doubts things of a superhuman origin or nature; has no premonitions, and disbelieves in them: p. 145.

VERY SMALL.—Has no spiritual guidings or superstitions: p. 146.

---

18. VENERATION.

DEVOTION; ADORATION of a Supreme Being; reverence for religion and things sacred; disposition to PRAY, WORSHIP, and observe religious rites. Adapted to the existence of a God, and the pleasures and benefits experienced by man in worshiping him. Perverted, it produces idolatry, bigotry religious intolerance, etc.

LARGE.—Experiences an awe of God and things sacred; loves to adore the Supreme Being, especially in his works; feels true devotion, fervent piety, and love of divine things; takes great delight in religious exercises; has much respect for superiority; regards God as the centre of hopes, fears, and aspirations; with large Hope and Spirituality, worships him as a spirit, and hopes to be with and like him; with large Ideality, contemplates his works with rapture and ecstacy; with large Sublimity, adores him as infinite in every thing; with large reasoning organs, has clear, and, if the faculties are unperverted, correct ideas of the Divine character and government, and delights to reason thereon; with large Philoprogenitiveness, adores him as a friend and father; and with large Benevolence, for his infinite *goodness*, etc.; with large Causality added, as securing the happiness of sentient beings by a wise institution of *law*, and as the great first CAUSE of all things; with large and perverted Cautiousness, mingles fear and dread with worship; with large Constructiveness and Causality, admires the system of his architectural plans, contrivances, etc.: p. 148.

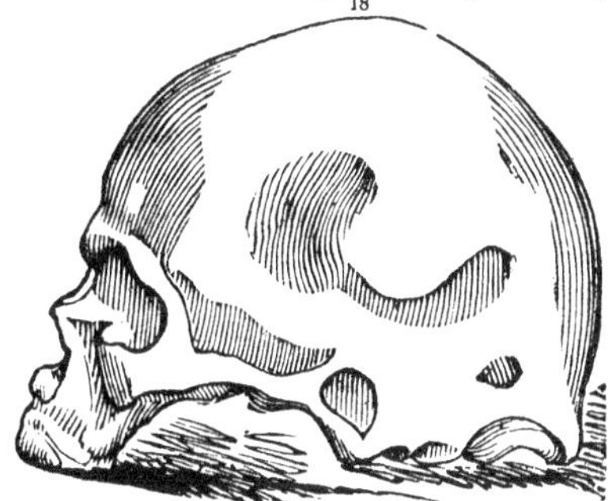

No. 75. LARGE.

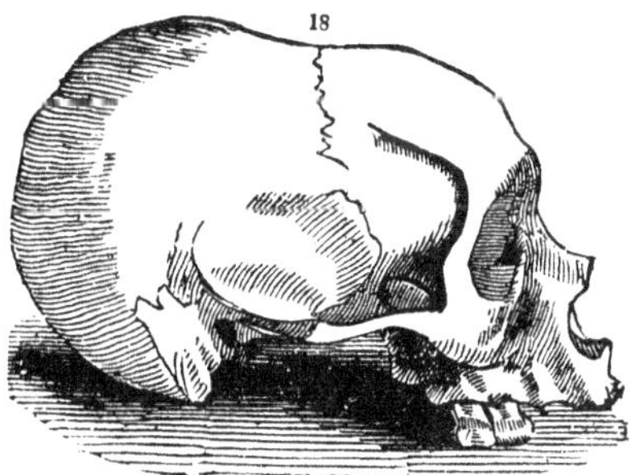

No. 76. SMALL.

VERY LARGE.—Experiences these feelings in a still higher degree; places God as supreme upon the throne of the soul, and makes his worship a central verge; manifests extreme fervor, anxiety, and delight in divine worship, and is pre-eminently fervent in prayer; with moderate Self-Esteem, and large Conscientiousness and Cautiousness, and a disordered temperament, experiences the utmost unworthiness and guiltiness in his sight, and is crushed by a sense of guilt and vileness, especially before God, yet should never cherish these feelings; is always dreading the wrath of Heaven, no matter whether the actions are good or ill; and should cultivate religious cheerfulness and hope of future happiness. For additional combinations, see large: p. 149.

FULL.—Experiences a good degree of religious worship, whenever circumstances excite this faculty, yet allows the larger faculties frequently to divert it, and prays at least internally; with large or very large Conscience or Benevolence, will place his religion in doing right and doing good, more than in religious observances; will esteem duties higher than ceremonies; with large propensities, may be devout upon the Sabbath, yet will be worldly through the week, and experience some conflict between his religious and his worldly aspirations: p. 149.

AVERAGE.—Will adore the Deity, yet often makes religion subservient to the larger faculties; with large Adhesiveness, Benevolence, and Conscience, may love religious meetings because it meets friends, and prays for the good of mankind, or because duty requires their attendance; yet is not habitually and innately devotional, except when this faculty is excited: p. 147.

MODERATE.—Will not be particularly devout or worshipful; with large Benevolence and Conscientiousness, if religiously educated, may be religious, yet will place religion more in works than faith, in duty than in prayer, and be more moral than pious; in his prayers will supplicate blessings upon mankind; and with Conscientiousness large, will confess sin more than express an awe of God; with large reflectives, can worship no further than it sees a *reason;* with moderate Spirituality and Conscientiousness, cares little for religion as such, but with large Benevolence, places religion mainly in doing good, etc.; and is by no means conservative in religion, but takes liberal views of religious subjects; and is religious only when this faculty is considerably excited: p. 150.

SMALL.—Experiences little devotion or respect, and is deficient in fervor; cares little for religious observances, and is not easily impressed with the worshiping sentiment: p. 150.

VERY SMALL.—Is almost destitute in feeling and practice of this sentiment.

19. BENEVOLENCE.

KINDNESS; HUMANITY; desire to make OTHERS happy; a SELF-SACRIFICING disposition; PHILANTHROPY; GENEROSITY; the ACCOMODATING, NEIGHBORLY spirit. Adapted to man's capability of making his fellow-men happy. Perversion—misplaced sympathies.

LARGE.—Delights to do good; makes personal sacrifices to make others happy; cannot witness pain or distress, and does what it well can to relieve them; manifests a perpetual flow of disinterested goodness; with large Adhesiveness, Ideality, and Approbativeness, and only average propensities and Self-Esteem, is remarkable for practical goodness; lives more for others than self; with large domestic organs, makes great sacrifices for family; with large reflectives, is perpetually reasoning on the evils of society, the way to obviate them, and to render mankind happy with large Adhesiveness is hospitable; with moderate Destructiveness cannot witness pain or death, and disapproves of capital punishment; with moderate Acquisitiveness, gives freely to the needy, and never exacts dues from the poor; with large Acquisitiveness, helps others to help themselves rather than gives money; with large Combativeness, Destructiveness, Self-Esteem, and Firmness, at times evinces harshness, yet is generally kindly disposed: p. 155.

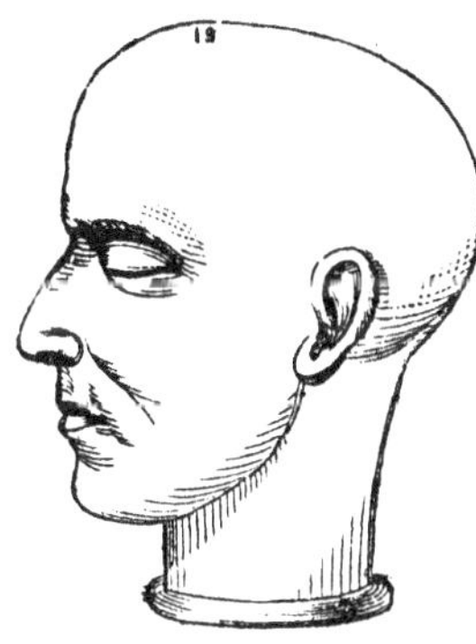

No. 77. Large. No. 78. Small.

Very Large.—Is deeply and thoroughly embued with a benevolent spirit; with large Adhesiveness and moderate Acquisitiveness, is too ready to help friends; and with large Hope added, especially inclined to endorse for them, which he should forswear not to do; with large Acquisitiveness, bestows time more freely than money, yet will also give the latter; but with only average or full Acquisitiveness freely bestows both substance and personal aid; with large Veneration and only full Acquisitiveness, gives freely to religious objects; with large Combativeness and Destructiveness, is more severe in word than deed, and threatens more than executes; with larger moral than animal organs, literally overflows with sympathy and practical goodness, and reluctantly causes others trouble; with large reasoning organs, is a true philanthropist, and takes broad views of reformatory measures; with large Adhesiveness and Philoprogenitiveness is pre-eminently qualified for nursing; with large Causality, is an excellent adviser of friends, etc., and should not let sympathy overrule judgment. See Benevolence large for additional combinations: p. 157.

FULL.—Shows a good degree of kind, neighborly, and humane feeling, except when the selfish faculties overrule it, yet is not remarkable for disinterestedness; with large Adhesiveness, manifests kindness toward friends; and with large Combativeness and Destructiveness, is unrelenting toward enemies; with large Acquisitiveness, is benevolent when it can make money thereby; with large Conscientiousness, is more just than kind, and with large Combativeness and Destructiveness, is unrelenting toward the offending: p. 158.

AVERAGE.—Manifests kindness only in conjunction with Adhesiveness and other large faculties; and with only full Adhesiveness, if kind is so for selfish purposes; with large Acquisitiveness, gives little or nothing, yet may sometimes do favors; with large Veneration, is more devout than humane; and with only full reasoning organs, is no philanthropist or reformer: p. 153.

MODERATE.—Allows the selfish faculties to infringe upon the happiness of others; with large Combativeness, Destructiveness, Self-Esteem, and Firmness, is comparatively hardened to suffering; and with Acquisitiveness and Secretiveness added, evinces almost unmitigated selfishness.

SMALL.—Cares little for the happiness of man or brute, and does still less to promote them; makes no disinterested self-sacrifices; is callous to human woe; does few acts of kindness, and those grudgingly, and has unbounded selfishness: p. 159.

VERY SMALL.—Feels little and evinces none of this sentiment, but is as selfish as the other faculties will allow him to be: p. 159.

---

20. CONSTRUCTIVENESS.

THE MAKING instinct; the TOOL-using talent; SLEIGHT of hand in constructing things. Adapted to man's need of things made, such as houses, clothes, and manufacturing articles of all kinds. Perverted, it wastes time and money on perpetual motion, and other like futile inventions.

LARGE.—Loves to make; is able to, and disposed to tinker, mend, and fix up, build, manufacture, employ machinery, etc.; shows mechanical skill and dexterity in whatever is done with the hands; with large Causality and perceptives, is given to inventing; and with large Imitation added, can make from a pattern, and both copy the improvements of others, and supply defects by its own inventions, as well as improve on the mechanical contrivances of others; with the mental temperament, and large intellectual organs and Ideality, employs ingenuity in constructing sentences and arranging words, and forming essays, sentiments, books, etc.: p. 161.

VERY LARGE.—Shows extraordinary ingenuity, and a perfect passion for making every thing; with large Imitation, Form, Size, and Locality, has first-rate talents as an artist, and for drawing, engraving, etc.; and with Color added, is an excellent limner; with Ideality, adds niceness to skill; with large Causality, adds invention to execution, etc.: p. 162.

No. 79. LARGE.

No. 80. SMALL.

FULL.—Can, when occasion requires, employ tools and use the hands in making, tinkering, and fixing up, and turn off work with skill, yet has no great natural passion or ability therein; with practice, can be a good workman; without it, would not excel: p. 163.

AVERAGE.—Like full, only less gifted in this respect: p. 160.

MODERATE.—Is rather awkward in the use of tools, and in manual operations of every kind; with large Causality and perceptives, shows more talent in inventing than executing, yet no great in either; with the mental temperament, evinces some mental construction, yet no great physical ingenuity: p. 163.

SMALL.—Is deficient in the tool-using capability; awkward in making and fixing up things; poor in understanding and managing machinery; takes hold of work awkwardly and wrong end first; writes poorly, and lacks both mental and physical construction: p. 163.

VERY SMALL.—Can make nothing, except in the most awkward manner: p. 163.

21. IDEALITY.

No. 81. LARGE.

No. 82. SMALL.

PERCEPTION and admiration of the BEAUTIFUL and perfect; good TASTE and refinement; PURITY of feeling; sense of PROPRIETY, ELEGANCE, and GENTILITY; POLISH and IMAGINATION. Adapted to the beautiful in nature and art. Perverted, it gives fastidiousness and extra niceness.

LARGE.—Appreciates and enjoys beauty and perfection wherever found, especially in nature; is graced by purity and propriety of expression and conduct; by gracefulness and polish of manners, and general good taste; is pure-minded; enjoys the ideal of poetry, elegance, and romance; longs after perfection of character, and desires to obviate blemishes, and with Conscientiousness large, moral imperfections; with large social organs, evinces a nice sense of propriety in friendly intercourse; with large Alimentiveness, eats in a becoming and genteel manner; with large moral organs, appreciates most highly perfection of character, or moral beauties and excellences; with large reflectives, adds a high order of sense and strength of mind to beauty and perfection of character; with large perceptives, is gifted with a talent for the study of nature, etc.: p. 166.

VERY LARGE.—Has a rich and glowing imagination and a very high order of taste and love of perfection; is disgusted with whatever is gross, vulgar or out of taste; with only average Causality, has more outside polish than solidity of mind; and more exquisiteness than sense: p. 167.

FULL.—Evinces a good share of taste and refinement, yet not a high order of them, except in those things in which it has been vigorously cultivated; with large Language, Eventuality, and Comparison may compose with elegance, and speak with much natural eloquence, yet will have more force of thought than beauty of diction; with large Constructiveness, will use tools with considerable taste, yet more skill; with large Combativeness and Destructiveness, shows general refinement, except when provoked, and is then grating and harsh; with large moral organs evinces more moral beauty and harmony than personal neatness; with large intellectual organs, possesses more beauty of mind than regard for looks and outside appearances, and prefers the sensible to the elegant and nice, etc.: p. 168.

AVERAGE.—Prefers the plain and substantial to the ornamental, and is a utilitarian; with large intellectual organs, prefers sound, solid matter to the ornament of style, and appreciates logic more than eloquence; with Benevolence and Adhesiveness large, is hospitable, and evinces true cordiality, yet cares nothing for ceremony; with Approbativeness large, may try to be polite, but makes an awkward attempt, and is rather deficient in taste and elegance; with Constructiveness large, makes things that are solid and serviceable, but does not polish them off; with Language large, talks directly to the purpose, without paying much attention to the mode of expression, etc.: p. 160.

MODERATE.—Rather lacks taste in manners and expression; has but little of the sentimental or finished; should cultivate harmony and perfection of character, and endeavor to polish up; with large propensities, evinces them in rather a coarser and grosser manner, and is more liable to their perverted action than when this faculty is large, and is homespun in every thing: p. 163.

SMALL.—Shows a marked deficiency in whatever appertains to taste and style, also to beau[illegible] and sentiment: p. 163.

VERY SMALL.—Is almost deficient in taste, and evinces none: p. 164.

B. SUBLIMITY.

PERCEPTION and appreciation of the VAST, ILLIMITABLE, ENDLESS, OMNIPOTENT, and INFINITE. Adapted to that infinitude which characterizes every department of nature. Perverted, it leads to bombast, and a wrong use of extravagant ideas.

LARGE.—Appreciates and admires the grand, sublime, vast, magnificent, and splendid in nature and art; admires and enjoys exceedingly mountain scenery, thunder, lightning, tempests, vast prospects, and all that is awful and magnificent, also the foaming, dashing cataract, a storm at sea; the lightning's vivid flash, and its accompanying thunder; the commotion of the elements, and the star-spangled canopy of heaven, and all manifestations of omnipotence and infinitude; with large Veneration, is particularly delighted by the infinite as appertaining to the Deity, and his attributes and works; and with large Time added, has unspeakably grand conceptions of infinitude as applicable to devotion, past and future, and to the character and works of the Deity; with large intellectual organs, takes a comprehensive view of subjects, and gives illimitable scope to his investigations and conceptions, so that they will bear being carried out to any extent; and with Ideality large, adds the beautiful and perfect to the sublime and infinite.

VERY LARGE.—Has a passion for the wild, romantic, and infinite. See large.

FULL.—Enjoys grandeur, sublimity, and infinitude quite well, and imparts considerable of this element to his thoughts, emotions, and expressions; evinces the same qualities as large, only in a less degree.

AVERAGE.—Possesses considerable of this element, when it is powerfully excited, yet under ordinary circumstances, only an ordinary share of it.

MODERATE.—Is rather deficient in the conception and appreciation of the illimitable and infinite; and with Veneration moderate, fails to appreciate this element in nature and her Author.

SMALL.—Shows a marked deficiency in this respect, and should earnestly cultivate it.

VERY SMALL.—Is almost destitute of these emotions and conceptions.

---

22. IMITATION.

ABILITY and disposition to COPY, TAKE PATTERN, and IMITATE. Adapted to man's requisition for doing, talking, acting, etc., like others. Perverted, it copies even their faults.

LARGE.—Has a great propensity and ability to copy and take pattern from others; do what is seen done; describes and acts out well; with large Language, gesticulates much; with large perceptives, requires to be shown but once; with large Constructiveness easily learns to use tools, and to make things as others make them; and with small Continuity added, is a jack-at-all-trades, and thorough in none; begins many things, but fails

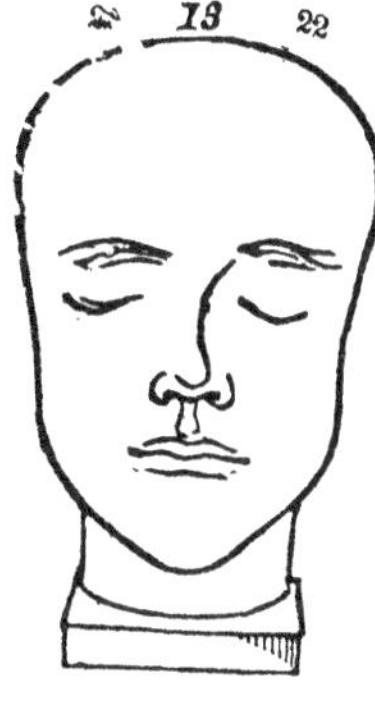

No. 83. LARGE.

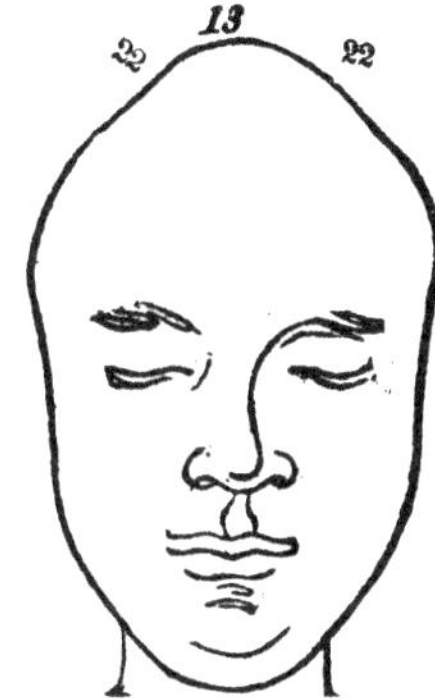

No. 84. SMALL.

a touch; with large Causality, perceptives, and an active temperament added, may make inventions or improvements, but never completes one till it makes another, or is always adding to them; with large Approbativeness, copies after renowned men; with large Adhesiveness, it takes pattern from friends; with large Language, imitates the style and mode of expression of others; with large Mirthfulness and full Secretiveness, creates laughter by taking off the oddities of people; with large Form, Size, and Constructiveness, copies shape and proportions; with large Color, imitates colors, and thus of all the other faculties: p. 170.

VERY LARGE.—Can mimic, act out, and pattern after almost any thing; with large Mirthfulness, relates anecdotes to the very life; has a theatrical taste and talent; gesticulates almost constantly while speaking; and, with large Language, imparts an uncommon amount of EXPRESSION to countenance, and every thing said; with large Individuality, Eventuality, Language, Comparison, and Ideality, can make a splendid speaker; and with large Mirthfulness, and full Secretiveness added, can keep others in a roar of laughter, yet remain serious; with an uneven head, is droll and humorous in the extreme; with large Approbativeness, delights in being the sport-maker at parties, etc., and excels therein; with large Constructiveness, Form, Size, Locality, and Comparison, full Color, and a good temperament, and a full-sized brain, can make a very superior artist of almost any kind; but with Color small, can engrave, draw, carve, model, etc., better than paint: p. 171.

FULL.—Copies quite well, yet not remarkably so; with large Causality, would rather invent a new way of doing things than copy the ordinary mode, and evinces considerable imitating talent when this faculty works in conjunction with large organs, but little otherwise: p. 171.

AVERAGE.—Can copy tolerably well when this faculty is strongly excited, yet is not a mimic, nor a natural copyist; with only full Constructiveness, evinces little manual dexterity; yet with large Causality, can originate quite well, and evinces no great disposition or ability to copy either the excellences or deficiencies of others, but prefers to be original: p. 169.

MODERATE.—Has little inclination to do what, and as, others do; but with large Causality, prefers to strike out a new course, and invent a plan of its own; with large Self-Esteem added, has an excellent conceit of that plan; but if Causality is only fair, is full of original devices, yet they do not amount to any great things: p. 171.

SMALL.—Copies even commonplace matter with extraordinary difficulty and reluctance; is original, and generally does every thing in its own way: p. 172.

VERY SMALL.—Possesses scarcely any, and manifests no disposition or ability to copy any thing, not even enough to learn to talk well: p. 172.

---

23. MIRTHFULNESS.

No. 85. LARGE. No. 86. SMALL.

INTUITIVE perception of the absurd and ridiculous; disposition and ability to joke and make fun, and laugh at what is improper, ill-timed, or unbecoming; pleasantness; facetiousness. Adapted to the absurd, inconsistent, and laughable. Pervert ed, it makes fun on solemn occasions, and where there is nothing ridiculous at which to laugh.

LARGE.--Enjoys a hearty laugh at the expressions and absurdities of others exceedingly, and delights to make fun out of every thing not exactly proper or in good taste, and is always ready to give as good a joke as it gets; with large Amativeness, loves to joke with and about the other sex, and with large Imitation and Langua[illegible] added, to talk with and tell stories to and about them; with large Combativeness and Ideality added, makes fun of their imperfections in dress, expression, manners, etc., and hits them off to admiration; with large Adhesiveness, Language, and Imitation is excellent company; with large Causality, Comparison, and Combativeness, argues mainly by ridicu[illegible] or by showing up the absurdity of the opposite side, and excels m[illegible] exposing the fallacy of other systems than in propounding its [illegible], with large Ideality, shows taste and propriety in its witticisms, [illegible] with this faculty average or less, is often gross, and with large Amativeness added, vulgar in jokes; with large Combativeness and Destructiveness, makes many enemies; and with large Comparison added, compares those disliked to something mean, disgusting, and ridiculous: p. 173.

VERY LARGE.—Shows an extraordinary disposition and capability to make fun; is always laughing and making others laugh; with large Language, Comparison, Imitation, Perceptives, and Adhesiveness, with moderate Self-Esteem and Secretiveness, is "the fiddle of the company;" with only average Ideality added, is clownish, and often says undignified and perhaps low things to raise a laugh, and with only moderate Causality, things that lack sense, etc.: p. 175.

FULL.—Possesses and evinces considerable of the fun-making disposition, especially in the direction of the larger organs; with large or very large Comparison, Imitation, and Approbativeness, and moderate Self-Esteem, manifests more of the laughable and witty than is really possessed; may make much fun and be called a wit; yet it will be owing more to what may be called drollery than pure wit; with moderate Secretiveness and Self-Esteem, and an excitable temperament, lets fly witty conceptions on the spur of the moment, and thus increases their laughableness by their being well timed, sudden, etc.: p. 175.

AVERAGE.—Is generally serious and sedate, except when this faculty is excited, yet then often laughs heartily, and evinces considerable wit; with large Individuality and Language, often says many laughable things, yet they owe their wit more to argument or the criticism they embody, than to this faculty: p. 172.

MODERATE.—Is generally serious, sedate, and sober, and with large Self-Esteem, stern and dignified, nor companionable except when Adhesiveness is large, and in company with intimate friends; with only average

Ideality and Imitation, is very poor in joking, has to expand witticisms, and thereby spoils them; has some witty ideas, yet lacks in perceiving and expressing them; fails to please others in witticisms, and with large Approbativeness and Combativeness, is liable to become angry when joked, and should cultivate this faculty by laughing and joking more: p. 176.

SMALL.—Makes little fun; is slow to perceive, and still slower to turn jokes; seldom laughs, and thinks it foolish or wrong to do so; with only average Adhesiveness, is uncompanionable; with large reflectives and Language, may do well in newspaper diction, yet not in debate: p. 177

VERY SMALL.—Has few, if any, witty ideas and conceptions: p. 177.

INTELLECTUAL FACULTIES.

KNOWING, REMEMBERING, and REASONING powers; general INTELLECTUAL CAPABILITY and desire. Adapted to the physical and metaphysical. Perverted, they apply their respective power to accomplish wrong ends.

LARGE.—Confer sufficient natural talent, and intellectual capability to take a high stand among men; give strength of mind, superior judgment, and power both of acquiring knowledge easily, and reasoning profoundly. Their direction depends upon the other faculties; with large animal organs and weak morals, they make philosophical sensualists; with large moral and weaker animal organs, moral and religious philosophers, etc.

VERY LARGE.—Give natural greatness of intellect and judgment, and a high order of natural talents; confer superior judgment and a high order of sound sense, with an original, capacious, comprehensive mind which can hardly fail to make its mark.

FULL.—Has good intellectual capabilities and much strength of mind, provided it is well cultivated; with large Acquisitiveness, a talent for acquiring property; with large moral organs, enlighten and improve the moral character; with large Constructiveness, give mechanical intelligence, etc.

AVERAGE.—Evinces fair mental powers, provided they are cultivated, otherwise only moderate intellectual capabilities; with an excitable temperament, allow the feelings and larger faculties to control judgment; with large moral organs, has more piety than talents, and allows religious prejudices and preconceived doctrines to prevent impartial intellectual examination; with moderate Acquisitiveness, will never acquire property with average Constructiveness, will be a poor mechanic, etc.

MODERATE.—Is rather deficient in sense and judgment, yet not palpably so; can be easily imposed upon; is deficient in memory, and rather wanting in judgment, comprehension, and intellectual capacity.

SMALL.—Is decidedly deficient in mind; slow and dull of comprehension; lacks sense, and has poor powers of memory and reason.

VERY SMALL.—Is a natural idiot.

These faculties are divided into the three following classes, which, when large, confer three kinds of talent.

SPECIES 1ST.—THE PERCEPTIVE FACULTIES.

These bring man into direct intercourse with the physical world; take cognizance of the physical qualities of material things; give practical judgment, and a practical cast of mind.

LARGE.—Judges correctly of the various qualities and relations of matter; with Acquisitiveness large, forms correct ideas of the value of property, goods, etc., and what kinds are likely to rise in value, and makes good bargains; with large Constructiveness, render important service in mechanical operations, and give very good talents for building machinery, superintending workmen, etc.; with the mental temperament and large intellectuals added, confer a truly scientific cast of mind, and a talent for studying the natural sciences, and are useful in almost every department and situation in life; with an active temperament and good general advantages, know a good deal about matters and things in general; give quickness of observation and perception and matter-of-fact, common-sense tact, and will show off to excellent advantage, appear to know all that they really do, perhaps more; confer a talent for acquiring and retaining knowledge with great facility, and attending to the details of business; becoming an excellent scholar, etc.; and give a strong thirst after knowledge.

VERY LARGE.—Are pre-eminent in these respects; know by intuition the proper conditions, fitness, value, etc., of things; power of observation, and ability to acquire knowledge, and a natural taste for examining; collecting statistics, studying the natural sciences, etc. For combinations see large.

FULL.—Confer fair perceptive powers, and a good share of practical sense; learns and remembers most things quite well; loves reading and knowledge, and with study can become a good scholar, yet not without it; with large Acquisitiveness, judge of the value of things with sufficient correctness to make good bargains, but with moderate Acquisitiveness, lacks such judgment; with large Constructiveness, aided by experience, confer a good mechanical mind, but without experience or only moderate Constructiveness are deficient in this respect, etc.

AVERAGE.—Confer only fair perceptive and knowing powers, but, well cultivated, know considerable about matters and things, and learn with tolerable ease; yet without cultivation are deficient in practicability of talent, and capability of gathering and retaining knowledge. For combinations see full.

MODERATE.—Are rather slow and dull of observation and perception, require some time to understand things, and even then lacks specificness and detail of knowledge; are rather deficient in matter-of-fact knowledge, and show off to poor advantage; learn slowly and fail in off-hand judgment and action; with only average Acquisitiveness, are deficient in judging of the value of things, and easily cheated; and with moderate Language, are rather wanting in practical talent, and cannot show advantageously what is possessed.

SMALL.—Is very deficient in remembering and judging; lacks practical sense, and should cultivate the knowing and remembering faculties.

VERY SMALL.—Sees few things, and knows almost nothing about the external world, its qualities, and relations.

---

24. INDIVIDUALITY.

No. 87. LARGE.

No. 88. SMALL.

OBSERVATION; desire to SEE and EXAMINE; cognizance of individual OBJECTS. Adapted to individual existence, or the THINGNESS of things; and is the door through which most forms of knowledge enter the mind. Perverted, makes the starer and the impudently observing.

LARGE.—Gives a great desire to see, know, examine, experience, etc.; is a great and practical observer of men and things; sees whatever is transpiring around, what should be done, etc.; is quick of perception. knowing; with large Acquisitiveness, is quick to perceive whatever appertains to property; with large Philoprogenitiveness, whatever concerns its children; with large Alimentiveness, whatever belongs to the flavor or qualities of food, and knows what things are good by looking at them; with large Approbativeness or Self Esteem, sees quickly whatever appertains to individual character, and whether it be favorable or unfavorable; with large Conscientiousness, perceives readily the moral, or right and wrong of things; with large Veneration, "sees God in clouds, and hears him in the winds;" with large Ideality, is quick to perceive beauty, perfection, and deformity; with large Form, notices the countenances and looks of all it meets; with small Color, fails to observe tints, hues, and shades; with large Order and moderate Ideality, perceives disarrangement at once, yet fails to notice the want of taste or niceness. These and kindred combinations show why some persons are very quick to notice some things, but slow to observe others: p. 184.

VERY LARGE.—Has an insatiable desire to see and know every thing, together with extraordinary powers of observation; cannot rest satisfied till it knows the whole; individualizes every thing, and is very minute and particular in its observation of things; with large Ideality, employs many allegorical and like figures; with large Human Nature and Comparison, observes every little thing which people say and do, and reads character correctly from what smaller Individuality would not notice: p. 185.

FULL.—Has good observing powers, and much desire to see and know things, yet is not remarkable in these respects; with large Acquisitiveness, but moderate Ideality, is quick to notice whatever appertains to property, yet fails to observe instances of beauty and deformity; but with large Ideality and moderate Acquisitiveness, quickly sees beauty and deformity, yet does not quickly observe the qualities of things or value of property; with large Philoprogenitiveness and Ideality, sees at once indices of beauty and perfection in children; but if Ideality and Language be moderate, fails to perceive beauty of expression or sentiment etc.: p. 185.

AVERAGE.—Observes only the more conspicuous objects around it, and these more in general than in detail, and what especially interests the larger faculties: p. 183.

MODERATE.—Is rather deficient in observing disposition and capability, and should cultivate this faculty; with large Locality, may observe places sufficiently to find them again; with large Order, observes when things are out of place; with large Causality, sees that it may find materials for reasoning, etc.: p. 185.

SMALL.—Observes only what is thrust upon his attention, and is quite deficient in this respect: p. 186.

VERY SMALL.—Sees scarcely any thing: p. 186.

25. FORM.

No. 89. LARGE.
FORM, SIZE, AND COLOR.

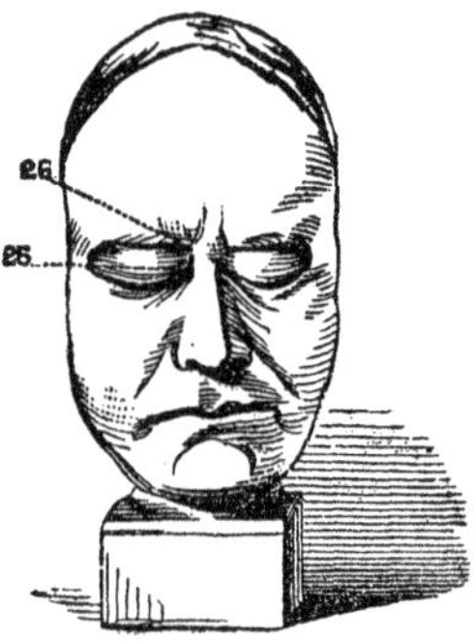

No. 90. SMALL.
FORM, SIZE, AND COLOR.

COGNIZANCE and recollection of SHAPE; memory of COUNTENANCES and the LOOKS of persons and things seen; perception of RESEMBLANCES, family likenesses, etc. Adapted to shape. Perverted, sees imaginary shapes of persons, things, etc.

LARGE.—Notices, and for a long time remembers, the faces, countenances, forms, looks, etc., of persons, beasts, and things once seen; knows by sight many whose name is not remembered; with Individuality large, both observes and recollects persons and things, but with Individuality moderate, fails to notice them, and hence to remember them, unless business or something special draws attention to them; with large Philoprogenitiveness, notices and recollects children, favorite animals, etc.; with large Acquisitiveness, Individuality, and Locality, readily detects counterfeits, etc.: p. 187.

VERY LARGE.—Possesses this capability in an extraordinary degree; recognizes persons not seen for many years; with large Ideality, takes extreme delight in beautiful forms; with large Spirituality, sees the spirits of the departed; with disordered nerves, sees horrid images, etc.: p. 188.

FULL—Has a good recollection of the countenances of persons and shape of things, yet not remarkably good unless this faculty has been quickened by practice, or invigorated by some strong incentive to its action; with large Ideality, will recollect beautiful shapes; with large Locality and Sublimity, beautiful and magnificent scenery, etc.; and should impress the recollection of shape upon the mind: p. 188.

AVERAGE.—Has only a fair natural recollection of shapes, countenances, etc.; yet with much practice may do tolerably well, but without practice will be comparatively deficient in these respects; and should cultivate this faculty: p. 186.

MODERATE.—Is rather deficient in recognizing persons before seen; fails to recognize by their looks those who are related to each other by blood, and should cultivate this faculty by trying to remember persons and things: p. 189.

SMALL.—Has a poor recollection of persons, looks, etc.; often meets persons the next day after an introduction, or an evening interview, without knowing them; with Eventuality large, may remember their history, but not their faces; with Locality large, where they were seen, but not their looks, etc.: p. 189.

VERY SMALL.—Manifests scarcely any of this faculty: p. 189

---

26. SIZE.

COGNIZANCE of BULK, MAGNITUDE, QUANTITY, PROPORTION, etc.; ability to measure by the EYE. Adapted to the absolute and relative magnitude of things. Perverted, it is pained by sligh; departures from proportion, or architectural inaccuracies.

LARGE.—Has an excellent eye for measuring angles, proportions, dis proportions, and departures therefrom; and with large Constructiveness, gives a good mechanical eye, and judges correctly of quantity in general; loves proportion, and is pained by disproportion; and is necessary to artisans, mechanics, all kinds of dealers, students, etc.: p. 190.

VERY LARGE.—Possesses this capability in an extraordinary degree, and is pained in the extreme by the sight of disproportion; can tell how wide, how far, how long, how much, etc., with very great accuracy; detects at once the texture and quality or fineness or coarseness of goods, and excels in judgment of property where bulk and value are to be estimated by the eye, and can dispense with instruments in measuring: p. 191.

FULL.—Possesses a good share of this eye-measuring power, yet is not remarkable; with practice, does well; without it, rather poorly; and does well in its accustomed business: p. 191.

AVERAGE.—Has a fair eye for judging of bulk, weight, by the size, etc., and with practice would do tolerably well in this respect: p. 190.

MODERATE.—Measures by the eye rather inaccurately, and has poor judgment of bulk, quantity, distance, and whatever is estimated by this faculty: p. 191.

SMALL.—Is obliged always to rely on actual measurements, because the eye is too imperfect to be trusted: p. 191.

VERY SMALL.—Is almost destitute of this faculty: p 192

---

27. WEIGHT.

INTUITIVE perception and application of the laws of GRAVITY, MOTION, etc. Adapted to man's requisition for motion. Perverted, it runs imminent risk of falling.

LARGE.—Has an excellent faculty for preserving and regaining balance; riding a fractious horse; skating; carrying a steady hand, etc.; easily keeps from falling when aloft, or in dangerous places; throws a stone, ball, or arrow straight; is pained at seeing things out of plumb; judges of perpendiculars very exactly; loves to climb, walk on the edge of a precipice, etc.; with Form and Size large, is an excellent marksman; with Constructiveness large, possesses an excellent faculty for understanding and working machinery; with Approbativeness large, is venturesome etc., to show what risks it can run without falling: p. 193.

VERY LARGE.—Possesses these capabilities in an extraordinary degree; is a dead shot; rarely ever falls, or is thrown from a horse: p. 194.

FULL.—Has a good degree of this faculty, and with practice excels, yet without it is not remarkable: p. 194.

AVERAGE.—Like full, only less gifted in this respect; with only average Constructiveness and perceptives, should never engage in working machinery, because deficient in this talent: p. 192.

MODERATE.—Can keep the balance under ordinary circumstances, yet has rather imperfect control over the muscles in riding a fractious horse, or walking a narrow beam aloft; with large Cautiousness, is timid in dangerous places, and dare not trust itself far; is not first-rate in skating, throwing, etc., unless rendered so by practice, and should cultivate this faculty by climbing, balancing, throwing, etc.: p. 194.

SMALL.—Is quite liable to sea-sickness, dizziness when aloft, etc., and naturally clumsy; with large Cautiousness, is afraid to walk over water, even on a wide plank, and where there is no danger; never feels safe while climbing, and falls easily: p. 195.

VERY SMALL.—Can hardly stand erect and has very little control over the muscles: p. 195.

---

28. COLOR.

PERCEPTION, recollection, and application, of COLORS, and DELIGHT in them. Adapted to that infinite variety of coloring interspersed throughout nature. Perverted, is over-particular to have colors just right.

LARGE.—Can discern and match colors by the eye with accuracy; with Comparison large, can compare them closely, and detect similarities and differences; with Constructiveness, Form, Size, and Imitation large or very large, can excel in painting; but with Form and Size only average, can paint better than draw; with Ideality large, is exceedingly delighted with fine paintings, and disgusted with imperfect coloring; with large Form and Size, manages the perspective of painting admirably: p. 195.

VERY LARGE.—Has a natural taste for painting; and with a large brain and very large Constructiveness, Imitation, Form, and Size, and large Weight, has a genius and passion for painting, and takes the utmost de light in viewing harmonious colors: p. 196.

FULL.—Possesses a good share of coloring ability and talent provided it has been cultivated; takes much pleasure in beautiful flowers, variegated landscapes, beautifully colored fruits, etc.: p. 196.

AVERAGE.—Possesses a fair share of this talent, yet is not extraordinary: p. 195.

MODERATE.—With practice, may judge of colors with considerable accuracy, yet without it will be somewhat deficient in this respect; with large Form, Size, Constructiveness, Ideality, and Imitation, may take an excellent likeness, yet will fail somewhat in the coloring: p. 197.

SMALL.—Can tell the primitive colors from each other, yet rarely notices the color of dress, eyes, hair, etc.; cannot describe persons and things by them, and evinces a marked deficiency in coloring taste and talent: p. 197.

VERY SMALL.—Can hardly tell one color from another, or form any idea of colors: p. 197

29. ORDER.

METHOD, SYSTEM, ARRANGEMENT. Adapted to Heaven's first law. Perverted, it overworks, and annoys others to keep things in order, and is tormented by disarrangement.

LARGE.—Has a desire to conduct business on methodical principles, and to be systematic in every thing; with large Acquisitiveness and Causality, has good business talents; with large Locality, has a place for every thing, and every thing in its place; with large Time, has a time for every thing, and every thing in season; with large Continuity, Comparison, and the mental temperament, has every idea, paragraph, and head of a subject in its proper place; with large Constructiveness, has its tools where it can always lay hands upon them in the dark; with large Combativeness, is excessively vexed by disarrangement; with large Language, places every word exactly right in the sentence; with large Approbativeness, is inclined to conform to established usages; with large Size, must have every thing in rows, or straight; and with large Ideality must have every thing neat and nice as well as methodical, etc.: p. 199.

VERY LARGE.—Is very particular about order, even to old maidishness; works far beyond strength to have things just so; and with large Ideality, and an active temperament, and only fair Vitality, is liable to break down health and constitution by overworking in order to have things extra nice, and takes more pains to keep things in order than this order is worth; with large Ideality, is fastidious about personal appearance, and extra particular to have every little thing very nice; and with Acquisitiveness added, cannot bear to have garments soiled, and is pained in the extreme by grease spots, ink blots, and like deformities: p. 199.

FULL.—If educated to business habits, evinces a good degree of method, and disposition to systematize, but without practice, may sometimes show laxity; with a powerful mentality, but weaker muscles, likes to have things in order, yet does not always keep them so; with large Causality added, shows more mental than physical order; with large moral organs, likes to have religious matters, codes of discipline, etc., rigidly observed, and has more moral than personal method; with Acquisitiveness and perceptives large, is sufficiently methodical for all practical business purposes, yet not extra particular: p. 200.

AVERAGE.—Likes order, yet may not always keep it, and desires more than it practically secures: p. 198.

MODERATE.—Is very apt to leave things where they were last used, and lacks method; with Ideality moderate, lacks personal neatness, and should cultivate this desirable element by being more particular: p. 201.

SMALL.—Has a very careless, inaccurate way of doing every thing leaves things where it happens; can never find what is wanted; takes a long time to get ready, or else goes unprepared, and has every thing in perpetual confusion: p 201.

VERY SMALL.—Is almost wholly destitute of this arranging power and desire: p. 201.

---

30. CALCULATION.

No. 91. LARGE.

No. 92. SMALL.

COGNIZANCE of NUMBERS; ability to reckon figures IN THE HEAD; MENTAL arithmetic. Adapted to the relations of numbers.

LARGE.—Excels in mental arithmetic, in adding, subtracting, multiplying, dividing, reckoning figures, casting accounts, etc., in the head; with large perceptives, has excellent business talents; and large Locality and Causality added, excels as a mathematician: p. 202.

VERY LARGE.—Possesses this calculating capability in a most extraordinary degree; can add several columns at once very rapidly and correctly, and multiply and divide with the same intuitive powers; loves mental arithmetic exceedingly well: p. 203.

FULL.—Possesses good calculating powers; with practice can calculate in the head or by arithmetical rules easily and accurately, yet without practice is not remarkable; with large Form, Size, Comparison, Causality, and Constructiveness, can be a good geometrician or mathematician, yet will do better in the higher branches than merely arithmetical: p. 204.

AVERAGE.—Can learn arithmetic and do quite well by practice, yet is not naturally gifted in this respect: p. 202.

MODERATE.—Adds, subtracts, divides, and calculates with extreme difficulty; with large Acquisitiveness and perceptives, will make a better salesman than book-keeper: p. 204.

SMALL.—Is dull and incorrect in adding, subtracting, dividing, etc., dislikes figuring; is poor in arithmetic, both practical and theoretical, and should cultivate this faculty: p. 205.

VERY SMALL.—Can hardly count, much less calculate: p. 205.

---

31. LOCALITY.

COGNIZANCE of PLACE; recollection of the LOOKS of places, roads, scenery, and the LOCATION of objects; WHERE on a page ideas are to be found, and position generally; the GEOGRAPHICAL faculty; desire to SEE places, and the ability to FIND them. Adapted to the arrangement of space and place. Perverted, it creates a cosmopolitic disposition, and would spend every thing in traveling.

LARGE.—Remembers the whereabout of whatever it sees; can carry the points of the compass easily in the head, and is lost with difficulty either in the city, woods, or country; desires to see places, and never forgets them; studies geography and astronomy with ease; and rarely forgets where things are seen; with Constructiveness, remembers the arrangement of the various parts of a machine; with Individuality, Eventuality, and Human Nature, loves to see men and things as well as places, and hence has a passion for traveling: p. 205.

VERY LARGE.—Always keeps a correct idea of the relative and absolute position, either in the deep forests or the winding street; cannot be lost; is perfectly enamored of traveling; has literally a passion for it: p. 206.

FULL.—Remembers places well, yet not extraordinarily so; can generally find the way, yet may sometimes be lost or confused; with large Eventuality, remembers facts better than places: p. 207.

AVERAGE.—Recollects places and positions seen several times, yet in city or roads is occasionally lost; has no great geographical talent, yet by study and practice can do tolerably well: p. 205.

MODERATE.—Recollects places rather poorly; dare not trust itself in strange places or large cities; is not naturally good in geography, and to excel in it must study hard; should energetically cultivate this faculty by localizing every thing, and remembering just how things are placed: p. 207.

SMALL.—Is decidedly deficient in finding places, and recollects them with difficulty even when perfectly familiar with them: p. 208.

VERY SMALL.—Must stay at home unless accompanied by others, because it cannot find the way back: p. 208.

LITERARY FACULTIES.

THESE collect information, anecdotes, and remember matters of fact and knowledge in general, and give what is called a good memory. Adapted to facts, dates, and the communication of ideas and feelings.

LARGE.—Render their possessor smart, knowing, and off-hand; enable him to show off to good advantage in society; with large Ideality, give brilliancy to talent.

VERY LARGE.—Is extraordinarily well informed, if not learned and brilliant; according to his means is a first-rate scholar; has a literal passion for literary pursuits, and a strong cast of mind.

FULL.—Give a fair, matter-of-fact cast of mind and knowing powers, fair scholarship, and a good general memory.

AVERAGE.—If cultivated, give a good general memory and store considerable knowledge; yet without cultivation only a commonplace memory, and no great general knowledge.

MODERATE.—Know much more than they can think of at the time, or can tell; with large reflective faculties, has more judgment than memory, and strength of mind than ability to show off.

SMALL OR VERY SMALL.—Has a poor memory of most things, and inferior literary capabilities.

---

32. EVENTUALITY.

MEMORY of FACTS; recollection of CIRCUMSTANCES, NEWS, OCCURRENCES, and historical, scientific, and passing EVENTS; what has been SAID, SEEN, HEARD, and once KNOWN. Adapted to ACTION, or those changes constantly occurring around or within us.

LARGE.—Has a clear and retentive memory of historical facts, general knowledge, what has been seen, heard, read, done, etc., even in detail; considering advantages, is well informed and knowing; desires to witness and institute experiments: find out what is and has been, and learn anecdotes, particulars, and items of information, and readily recalls to mind what has once entered it; has a good general matter-of-fact memory, and picks up facts readily; with Calculation and Acquisitiveness, remembers business matters, bargains, etc.; with large social feelings, recalls friends to mind, and what they have said and done; and with large Locality, associates facts with the place where they transpired, and is particularly fond of reading, lectures, general news, etc., and can become a good scholar: p. 210.

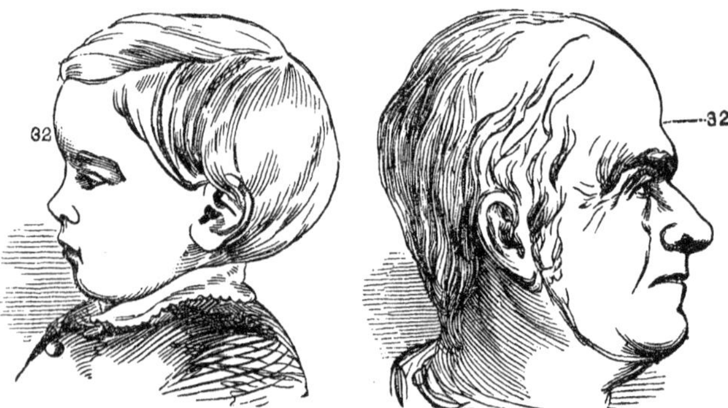

No. 93. LARGE No. 94. SMALL.

VERY LARGE.—Possesses a wonderfully retentive memory of every thing like facts and incidents; with large Language and Imitation, tells a story admirably, and excels in fiction, etc.; has a craving thirst for knowledge, and literally devours books and newspapers, nor allows any thing once in the mind to escape it: p. 211.

FULL.—Has a good general memory of matters and things, yet it is considerably effected by cultivation, that is, has a good memory if it is habitually exercised—if not, only an indifferent one; with large Locality, recollects facts by associating them with the place, or by recollecting where on a page they are narrated; with large reflectives, remembers principles better than facts, and facts by associating them with their principles; and with large Language, tells a story quite well: p. 212.

Average.—Recollects leading events and interesting particulars, yet is rather deficient in memory of items and details, except when it is well cultivated: p. 209.

Moderate.—Is rather forgetful, especially in details; and with moderate Individuality and Language, tells a story very poorly; and should cultivate memory by its exercise: p. 212.

Small.—Has a treacherous and confused memory of circumstances; often forgets what is wanted, what was intended to be said, done, etc.; has a poor command of knowledge, and should strenuously exercise this remembering power: p. 213.

Very Small.—Forgets almost every thing, both generals and particulars: p. 213.

---

33. TIME.

Cognizance and recollection of duration and succession; the lapse of time, when things occurred, etc., and ability to carry the time of the day in the head punctually. Adapted to periodicity. Perverted, it is excessively pained by bad time in music, not keeping steps in walking, etc.

Large.—Can generally tell when things occurred, at least the order of events and the length of time between one occurrence and another, etc.; tells the time of day without timepiece or sun, well; and keeps an accurate chronology in the mind, of dates, general and particular; with large Eventuality, rarely forgets appointments, meetings, etc.; and is a good historian: p. 215.

Very Large.—Can tell the time of day almost as correctly as with a timepiece, and the time that transpired between one event and another, and is a natural chronologist: p. 216.

Full.—With cultivation, can keep time in music, and also the time of day in the head quite correctly; yet not exceedingly so: p. 216.

Average.—With practice, has a good memory of dates and successions, yet without it is rather deficient: p. 214.

Moderate.—Has a somewhat imperfect idea of time and dates; with moderate Individuality, Eventuality, and Language, is a poor historian: p. 216.

Small.—Has a confused and indistinct idea of the time when things transpired, and forgets dates: p. 217.

Very Small.—Is almost wholly destitute of this faculty: p. 217.

34. TUNE

ABILITY to learn and remember tunes BY ROTE; the MUSIC instinct and faculty. Adapted to the musical octave. Perversion—excessive fondness for music to the neglect of other things.

LARGE.—Loves music dearly; has a nice conception of concord, discord, melody, etc., and enjoys all kinds of music; and with large Imitation, Constructiveness, and Time, can make most kinds, and play well on musical instruments; with large Ideality, imparts a richness and exquisiteness to musical performances; has a fine taste and is tormented by discord, but delighted by concord, and takes a great amount of pleasure in the exercise of this faculty; with large Combativeness and Destructiveness, loves martial music; with large Veneration, sacred music; with large Adhesiveness and Amativeness, social and parlor music; with large Hope, Veneration, and disordered nerves, plaintive, solemn music, etc.: p. 218.

VERY LARGE.—Possesses extraordinary musical taste and talent, and is literally transported by good music; and with large Imitation and Constructiveness, fair Time, and a fine temperament, is an exquisite performer; learns tunes by hearing them sung once; sings in spirit and with melting pathos; shows intuitive taste and skill; sings *from* the soul *to* the soul: p. 219.

FULL.—Has a good musical ear and talent; can learn tunes by rote quite well; and with large Ideality, Imitation, and Firmness, can be a good musician, yet will require practice: p. 220.

AVERAGE.—Has fair musical talents, yet, to be a good musician, requires considerable practice; can learn tunes by rote, yet with some difficulty; with large Ideality and Imitation, may be a good singer or player, yet is indebted more to art than nature, shows more taste than skill, and loves music better than can make it: p. 217.

MODERATE.—Has no great natural taste or talent for music, yet, aided by notes and practice, may sing and play quite well, but will be rather mechanical; lacks that pathos and feeling which reaches the soul: p. 220.

SMALL.—Learns to sing or play tunes with great difficulty, and that mechanically, without emotion or effect: p. 221.

VERY SMALL.—Has scarcely any musical idea or feeling, so little as hardly to tell Yankee Doodle from Old Hundred: p. 221.

35. LANGUAGE.

No. 95. LARGE.

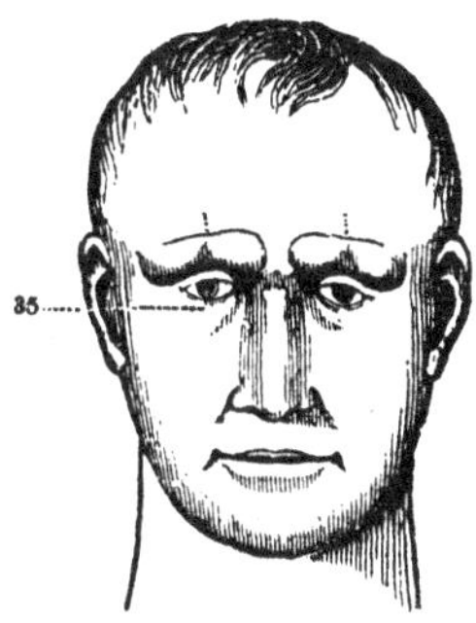
No. 96. SMALL.

EXPRESSION of ideas and feelings by words, written or spoken, gesture, looks, and action; the COMMUNICATIVE faculty and instinct in general. Adapted to man's requisition for holding communication with man. Perverted, it creates garrulity, excessive talkativeness, telling what does harm, etc.

LARGE.—Expresses ideas and feelings well, both verbally and in writing; can learn to speak languages easily; recollects words and commits to memory well; gives freedom, copiousness, and power of expression; with large Amativeness, uses tender, winning, persuasive words; with large Combativeness and Destructiveness, severe and cutting expressions; with large moral faculties, words expressive of moral sentiments; with large Acquisitiveness, describes in glowing colors what is for sale; with large Ideality, employs richness and beauty of expression, and loves poetry and oratory exceedingly; with large Imitation, expresses thoughts and emotions by gesticulation; with activity great and Secretiveness small, shows in the looks, thoughts, and feelings what is passing in the mind; with large reflective faculties, shows thought and depth in the countenance; with large Comparison, uses just the words which convey the meaning intended; with large mentality, activity, Ideality, Individuality, Eventuality, and Comparison, can make an excellent editor or newspaper writer; and with large Causality added, a philosophical writer: p. 224.

VERY LARGE.—Possesses the communicative disposition and faculty in an extraordinary degree; with activity and intellectuality great, throws an extraordinary amount of feeling and soul into every expression and action; is a natural linguist, and as fond of talking and writing as of eating; with activity great, average Causality, large Combativeness, and a nervous temperament, will be a scold: p. 226.

FULL.—Says well what it has to say, yet is not garrulous; with small Secretiveness, says without qualification, and also distinctly and pointedly; expresses the manifestations of the larger faculties with much force, yet not of the smaller ones; with large Secretiveness and Cautiousness, does not always speak to the purpose, and make itself fully understood, but uses rather non-committal expressions; with large Comparison, Human Nature, Causality, Ideality, activity, mentality, and power, has first-rate writing talents, and can speak well, yet large Secretiveness impairs speaking and writing talents by rendering them wordy and non-committal: p. 227.

AVERAGE.—Has fair communicating talents, yet not extra; with activity great and Secretiveness small, speaks right out and to the purpose, yet is not eloquent, and uses commonplace words and expressions; with large Individuality, Eventuality, and Comparison, and moderate Secretiveness, can make an excellent writer by practice; uses none too many words, but expresses itself clearly and to the point; with large Causality, has more thought than language; with moderate Individuality and Eventuality, finds it difficult to say just what it would, and is not fully and easily understood; with large Ideality, has more beauty and elegance than freedom: p. 222.

MODERATE.—Is not particularly expressive in words, actions, and countenance, nor ready in communicating ideas and sentiments; with large Ideality, Eventuality, Comparison, activity, and power, can succeed well as a writer, yet not as a speaker; with large Causality and moderate Eventuality, has abundance of thoughts, but finds it quite difficult to cast them into sentences, or bring in the right adjectives and phrases; is good in matter, yet poor in delivery; commits to memory with difficulty, and fails to make ideas and feelings fully understood, and to excite like organs in others; with large Eventuality, Locality, Form, and Comparison, may be a fair linguist, and learn to read foreign languages, yet learns to speak them with difficulty, and is barren in expression, however rich in matter: p. 228.

SMALL.—Has poor lingual and communicative talents; hesitates for words; speaks with extreme difficulty and very awkwardly, and should cultivate this faculty by talking and writing much: p. 228.

VERY SMALL.—Can hardly remember or use words at all, or even remember their meaning: p. 228.

REFLECTIVE OR REASONING FACULTIES.

THESE give a PHILOSOPHIZING, PENETRATING, INVESTIGATING, ORIGINATING cast of mind; ascertain CAUSES and abstract RELATIONS; CONTRIVE, INVENT, ORIGINATE ideas, etc. Adapted to the first principles or laws of things.

LARGE.—Confer the higher capabilities of intellect; reason clearly and strongly on whatever data is furnished by the other faculties; give soundness of understanding, depth of intellect, and that weight which carries conviction, and contribute largely to success in every thing; with perceptives small, possess more power of mind than can be manifested, and fails to be appreciated and understood, because more theoretical than practical.

VERY LARGE.—Possess extraordinary depth of reason and strength of understanding; and with large perceptives, extraordinary talents, and manifests them to good advantage; with perceptives small, gives great strength of understanding, yet a poor mode of manifesting it; are not appreciated, and lack balance of mind, and are more plausible than reliable, and too dark to be clear.

FULL.—Possess fair reflective powers, and reason well from the data furnished by the other faculties; and with activity great, have a fair flow of ideas and good general thoughts.

AVERAGE.—Reason fairly on subjects fully understood, yet are not remarkable for depth or clearness of idea; with cultivation, will manifest considerable reasoning power, without it only ordinary.

MODERATE.—Are rather deficient in power and soundness of mind; but with large perceptives, evince less deficiency of reason than is possessed.

SMALL.—Have inferior reasoning capabilities.

VERY SMALL.—Are almost wholly deficient in thought, idea, and comprehensiveness of mind.

---

36. CAUSALITY.

PERCEPTION and application of CAUSES; adaptation of ways and means to ends. Adapted to the institution in nature of causes and effects. Perverted by selfishness, it reasons in favor of untruth, and attains injurious ends.

6

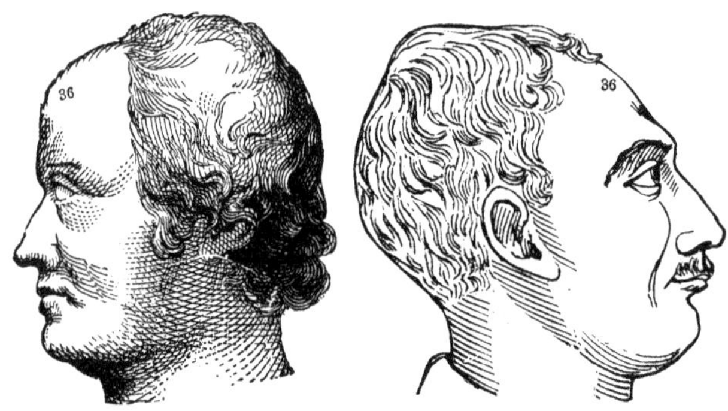

No. 97. LARGE. No. 98. SMALL.

LARGE.—Desires to know the WHY and WHEREFORE of things, and to investigate their LAWS; reasons clearly and correctly from causes to effects, and from facts to their causes; gives uncommon capabilities of planning, contriving, inventing, creating resources, and making the head save the hands; kills two birds with one stone; predicts results, and arranges things so as to succeed; synthetizes, and puts things together well; with large Combativeness, loves to argue; with large perceptives, will be quick to perceive facts and conditions, and reason powerfully and correctly from them; with Comparison and Conscientiousness large, reasons forcibly on moral truths; with the selfish faculties strong, will so adapt ways and means as to serve personal purposes; with moderate perceptives, will excel more in principles and philosophy than facts, and remember laws better than details; with Comparison and Human Nature large, is particularly fond of mental philosophy, and excels therein; with Individuality and Eventuality only moderate, will be guided more by reason than experience, by laws than facts, and arrive at conclusions more from reflection than observation; with large perceptives, possesses a high order of practical sense and sound judgment; with large Comparison and moderate Eventuality, remembers thoughts, inferences, and subject matter, but forgets items; with the mental temperament and Language moderate, will make a much greater impression upon mankind by action than expressions, by deeds than words, etc.: p. 233.

VERY LARGE.—Possesses this cause-seeking and applying power in an extraordinary degree; perceives by intuition those deeper relations of things which escape common minds; is a profound philosopher and a deep and powerful reasoner, and has great originality of mind and strength of understanding: p. 23[illegible].

Full.—Has good cause-seeking and applying talents; reasons and adapts ways and means to ends well; with large perceptives, Comparison, activity, and thought, possesses excellent reasoning powers, and shows them to first-rate advantage; with moderate perceptives and large Secretiveness, can plan better than reason; with large Acquisitiveness and moderate Constructiveness, lays excellent money-making, but poor mechanical plans, etc.: p. 236.

Average.—Plans and reasons well in conjunction with the larger faculties, but poorly with the smaller ones; with moderate Acquisitiveness, lays poor money-making plans; but with large Conscientiousness, reasons well on moral subjects, especially if Comparison be large, etc.: p. 231.

Moderate.—Is rather deficient in discerning and applying causes; perceives them when presented by other minds, yet does not originate them; with activity and perceptives large, may do well in the ordinary routine of business, yet fails in difficult matters: p. 237.

Small.—Is deficient in reasoning and planning power; needs perpetual telling and showing; seldom arranges things beforehand, and then poorly; should work under others; lacks force of idea and strength of understanding: p. 238.

Very Small.—Is idiotic in reasoning and planning: p. 238.

---

37. COMPARISON.

Inductive reasoning; ability and disposition to classify, compare, draw inferences from analogy, etc. Adapted to those classifications which pervade universal nature. Perverted, is too redundant in proverbs, fables, and figures of speech.

Large.—Reasons clearly and correctly from conclusions and scientific facts up to the laws which govern them; discerns the known from the unknown, detects error by its incongruity with facts; has an excellent talent for comparing, explaining, expounding, criticising, exposing, etc.; employs similes and metaphors well; puts this and that together, and draws inferences from them; with large Continuity uses well-sustained figures of speech, but with small Continuity, drops the figure before it is finished; with large Individuality, Eventuality, activity, and power, gives a scientific cast of mind; with large Veneration, reasons about God and his works; with large Language, uses words in their exact signification; with large Mirthfulness, hits the nail upon the head in all its criticisms, and hits off the oddities of people to admiration; with large Ideality gives beauty, taste, propriety of expression, etc.: p. 241.

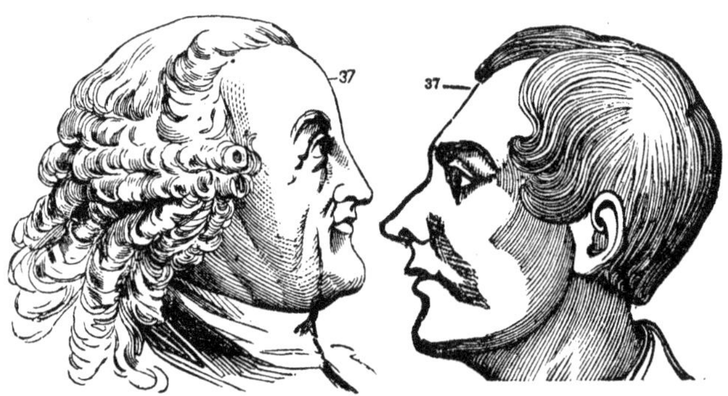

No. 99. Large. No. 100. Small.

Very Large.—Possesses this analyzing, criticising, and inductive faculty in a truly wonderful degree; illustrates with great clearness and facility from the known to the unknown; discovers the deeper analogies which pervade nature, and has an extraordinary power of discerning new truths; with large Individuality, Eventuality, and activity, has a great faculty of making discoveries; with large Language, uses words in their exact meaning, and is a natural philologist; with full Language, explains things plausibly and correctly: p. 243.

Full.—Possesses a full share of clearness and demonstrative power, yet with large Causality and only moderate Language, cannot explain to advantage; with large Eventuality, reasons wholly from facts; with moderate Language, fails in giving the precise meaning to words; and makes good analytical discriminations: p. 243.

Average.—Shows this talent in a good degree in conjunction with the larger faculties; but is rather wanting in reference to the smaller ones: p. 239.

Moderate.—Rather fails in explaining, clearing up points, putting things together, drawing inferences, and even uses words incorrectly; with Individuality and Eventuality moderate, shows much mental weakness; with large Causality, has good ideas, but makes wretched work in expressing them, and cannot be understood; with Mirthfulness full or large, tries to make jokes, but they are always ill-timed and inappropriate: p. 244.

SMALL.—Has a poor talent for drawing inferences; lacks appropriateness in every thing, and should cultivate this faculty: p. 244.

VERY SMALL—Has little, and shows almost none of this element p. 244.

C. HUMAN NATURE.

DISCERNMENT of CHARACTER; perception of MOTIVES; INTUITIVE physiognomy. Adapted to man's need of knowing his fellow-men. Perverted, it produces suspiciousness.

LARGE.—Reads men intuitively from their looks, conversation, manners, and walk, and other kindred signs of character; with Individuality and Comparison large, notices all the little things they do, and founds a correct estimate upon them, and should follow first impressions touching persons; with full Secretiveness and large Benevolence added, knows just how to take men, and possesses much power over mind; with Mirthfulness and Ideality large, sees all the faults of people, and makes much fun over them; with Comparison large, has a turn for metaphysics, etc.

VERY LARGE.—Possesses this faculty in an extraordinary degree; reads every body right through at first sight. For combinations see large.

FULL.—Reads character quite well from the face or external signs, yet is sometimes mistaken; may generally follow first impressions safely; loves to study character; with Ideality and Adhesiveness large, the excellences of friends; with Philoprogenitiveness large, of children; with Combativeness large, all the faults of people; and with only average Adhesiveness, forms few friendships, because it detects so many blemishes in character, etc.

AVERAGE.—Has fair talents for reading character, yet is not extra in this respcet, and may safely cultivate it.

MODERATE.—Fails somewhat in discerning character; occasionally forms wrong conclusions concerning people; should be more suspicious, watch people closely, especially those minor signs of character dropped when off their guard; has ill-timed remarks and modes of addressing people, and often says and does things which have a different effect from that intended.

SMALL.—Is easily imposed upon by others; with large Conscientiousness and small Secretiveness, thinks every body tells the truth; is too confiding, and fails sadly in knowing where and how to take things.

VERY SMALL—Knows almost nothing about human nature.

D. AGREEABLENESS.

Persuasiveness, pleasantness, blandness. Adapted to please and win others.

Large.—Has a pleasing, persuasive, conciliatory mode of addressing people, and of saying things; with Adhesiveness and Benevolence large, is generally liked; with Comparison and Human Nature large, says unacceptable things in an acceptable manner, and sugars over expressions and actions.

Very Large.—Is peculiarly winning and fascinating in manners and conversation, and wins over even opponents.

Full.—Is pleasing and persuasive in manner, and with Ideality large, polite and agreeable, except when the repelling faculties are strongly excited; with small Secretiveness and strong Combativeness and activity, is generally pleasant, but when angry is sharp and blunt; with large Benevolence, Adhesiveness, and Mirthfulness, is excellent company.

Average.—Has a good share of pleasantness in conversation and appearance, except when the selfish faculties are excited, but is then repulsive.

Moderate.—Is rather deficient in the pleasant and persuasive, and should by all means cultivate this faculty by sugaring over all it says and does.

Small.—Says even pleasant things very unpleasantly, and fails sadly in winning the good graces of people.

Very Small.—Is almost totally deficient in this faculty

RULES

FOR FINDING THE ORGANS.

PRE-EMINENTLY is Phrenology a science of FACTS. Observation discovered it—observation must perfect it; observation is the grand instrumentality of its propagation. To be convinced of its truth, nine hundred and ninety-nine men out of every thousand require to SEE it—to be convinced by INDUCTION, founded upon experiment. Hence the importance of giving definite RULES for finding the organs, by which even disbelievers may test the science, and believers be confirmed in its truth, and advanced in its study.

The best mode of investigating its truth, is somewhat as follows: You know a neighbor who has extreme Firmness in character; who is as inflexible as the oak, and as obstinate as the mule. Now, learn the location of the phrenological organ of Firmness, and apply that location to his head—that is, see whether he has this organ as conspicuous as you know him to have this faculty in character; and if you find a coincidence between the two, you have arrived at a strong phrenological fact.

You know another neighbor who is exceedingly cautious, timid, safe wise, and hesitating; who always looks at the objections and difficulties in the way of a particular measure, instead of at its advantages; who always takes abundant time to consider, and is given to procrastination Learn the location of Cautiousness, and see whether he has this phrenological organ as conspicuous as you know this faculty to exist in his character. By pursuing such a course as this, you can soon arrive at a sure knowledge of the truth or falsity of phrenological science; and this is altogether the best mode of convincing unbelievers of its truth, by means of the marked coincidence between the Phrenology and character of those they know; and it is not possible for the human mind to resist proof like this.

To promote this practical knowledge—the application of this science—we give the following RULES FOR FINDING the organs, fully assured that we can fill our pages with nothing more interesting or useful. Follow these rules exactly, and you will have little difficulty in finding at leas all the prominent organs.

Your first observation should be made upon TEMPERAMENT, or organ ization and physiology, with this principle for your basis: that when bodily texture or form is coarse, or strong, or fine, or soft, or weak, or sprightly, the texture of the brain will correspond with that of body, and the mental characteristics with that of brain. Still, it is not now our purpose to discuss the influence of various temperaments upon the direction of the faculties.

The second observation should be to ascertain what faculties CONTROL the character, or what is the dominant motive, desire, object, or passion of the person examined; in phrenological language, what faculties predominate in action: and it should here be observed, that the relative size of organs does not always determine this point. Some faculties, though very dominant in power, cannot. in their very nature, constitute a motive for action, but are simply executive functions, simply carrying into effect the dominant motives. For example, Combativeness rarely ever becomes a distinct motive for action. Few men love simply to wrangle, quarrel, and fight for fun, but they exercise Combativeness merely as a means of obtaining the things desired by the other dominant faculties. Few men have for their motive the mere exercise of will—that is, Firmness is generally exercised to carry into effect the design of the other faculties; and instead of subjecting the other faculties to itself, simply keeps them at their work, whatever that work may be. And thus of some other faculties. But Amativeness, Friendship, Appetite, Acquisitiveness, Benevolence, Veneration, Conscientiousness, or Intellect, Constructiveness, Ideality, or the observing faculties, may all become dominant motives. And it requires much phrenological shrewdness to ascertain what single faculty, cluster, or combination of faculties, leads off the character.

Let us take, then, for our starting point, the outer angle of the eye, and draw a line to the middle of the top of the ears, and DESTRUCTIVENESS is exactly under this point, and it extends upward about half an inch above the top of the ears, and in proportion to its size will the head be wide between the ears. And if Secretiveness be small and Destructiveness large, there will be a horizontal ridge extending forward and backward, more or less prominent, according to the size of this organ.

Three quarters of an inch above the middle of the top of the ears, SECRETIVENESS is located When this organ is large, it rarely gives a distinct projection, but simply fills and rounds out the head at this point. When the head widens rapidly from the junction of the ears as you rise upward, Secretiveness is larger than Destructiveness; but when the head becomes narrower as you rise, it is smaller than Destructiveness.

To find these two organs, and their relative size, place the third fingers of each hand upon the head just at the top of the ears; let the lower side of the third finger be even with the upper part of the ear; that finger then rests upon Destructiveness. Then spread the second finger about one eighth of an inch from the other, and it will rest upon Secretiveness

Let the end of your longest finger come as far forward as the fore part of the ears, and they will then rest upon these two organs.

Take, next, this same line, starting from the outer angle of the eye, to the top of the ears, and extend it straight backward an inch and a half to an inch and three quarters, and you are on Combativeness. This organ starts about midway to the back part of the ears, and runs upward and backward toward the crown of the head. To ascertain its relative size, steady the head with one hand, say the left, and place the balls of your right fingers upon the point just specified. letting your elbow be somewhat below the subject's head, which will bring your fingers directly ACROSS the organ. Its size may be ascertained partly from the general fullness of the head, and partly from its sharpness, according as the organ is more or less active; yet observers sometimes mistake this organ for the mastoid process directly behind the lower part of the ears. Remember our rule, namely: a line drawn from the outer angle of the eye to the top of the ear, and continued an inch and a half or three quarters straight back. Follow that rule, and you cannot mistake the position of this organ; and will soon, by comparing different heads, be able to arrive at those appearances when large or small.

To find PHILOPROGENITIVENESS, extend this line straight back to the middle of the back head, and you are on the organ; and in proportion as the head projects backward behind the ears at this point, will Philoprogenitiveness be larger or smaller.

About an inch, or a little less, directly BELOW this point, is the organ which controls MUSCULAR MOTION; and in proportion as this is more or less prominent, will the muscular system be more or less active. Those who have this prominence large, will be restless, always moving a hand or foot when sitting, and even when sleeping; will be light-footed, easy-motioned, fond of action, and willing to work, and possessed of a first-rate constitution. But when that prominence is weak, they will be found less fond of physical action and labor.

To return to Philoprogenitiveness. Three fourths of an inch ABOVE this point, INHABITIVENESS is located. When this organ is large, and Continuity is moderate, there will be found a prominence somewhat resembling an angle of a triangle, with the angle at the middle of the head, together with a sharp prominence at this point, But when Inhabitiveness is small, there will be a depression just about large enough to receive the end of a finger, with the bow downward. An inch on each side of this point is ADHESIVENESS. Or thus: taking the backward termination of that line already drawn, erect upon it a right-angle triangle; let the right angle be on Philoprogenitiveness, and the two sides which inclose this angle be about an inch and a half or three quarters each, and the other two angles will be on the two lobes of Adhesiveness—the hypothenuse, or long side, being about two inches, or two and a half inches, in length. When Adhesiveness is large—especially if Inhabitiveness and Continuity be small—there will be found two swells, somewhat resembling the larger end of an egg; but if small, the head will retire at this point.

Directly above Inhabitiveness and Adhesiveness, CONTINUITY is located When small, a depression resembling a new moon, with the horns turning DOWNWARD, surrounding the organs of Inhabitiveness and Adhesiveness, will be found. When Continuity is large, however, there will be no depression, nor any swell, but simply a FILLING OUT of the head at this point.

AMATIVENESS may be found thus: Take the middle of the back part of the ears as your starting point; draw a line backward an inch and a half, and you are upon this organ. Yet the outer portion next to the ear probably exercises the more gross and animal function of this faculty, while the inner portion takes on a more spiritual tone.

To find CAUTIOUSNESS, take the back or posterior part of the ears as your starting point; draw a perpendicular line, when the head is erect, from the extreme back part of the ear, straight up the side of the head, and just where the head begins to round off to form the top, Cautiousness is located. This organ is generally well developed in the American head, and those swells, generally seen at this point, are caused by a full development of this faculty.

To find ALIMENTIVENESS. take the upper and forward junction of the ear with the head as your starting point; draw a line half an inch forward, inclining a little downward, and you are upon this organ. Then rise three quarters of an inch straight upward, and you are on that part of ACQUISITIVENESS which gets property. Yet a better rule for finding it is this: Find Secretiveness in accordance with the rule already given, and Acquisitiveness is three quarters of an inch FORWARD of the point, and about an inch above the middle of the tip of the ear. Or thus: Take the middle of the top of the ear as your starting point; draw a perpendicular line three quarters of an inch upward, and you are on Secretiveness; and then about an inch forward, and you are on Acquisitiveness. The back part of Acquisitiveness seeks partnership and ACQUIRES, while the fore part HOARDS money. When the head widens rapidly as you pass from the outer angles of the eyes to the top of the ears, Acquisitiveness is large; but when the head is thin in this region, Acquisitiveness is small.

SUBLIMITY, IDEALITY, and CONSTRUCTIVENESS, can be found by the following rule: First find Cautiousness by applying the rule already laid down for that purpose, then pass directly forward an inch, and you are on Sublimity; extend this line on another inch, and you are on Ideality; then an inch downward brings you upon Constructiveness.

It should be remembered that Cautiousness, Sublimity, and Ideality are just upon the turning of the head, or between the top and the sides of the head Usually the head is much wider at Cautiousness than at Subtimity, and at Sublimity than Ideality. When, however, the head is as wide at Ideality as at Cautiousness, the subject will be found possessed of unusual good taste, purity, refinement, elevation, and personal perfection. Half an inch forward of Ideality is the organ which appertains to dress, and secures personal neatness. In those who care but little what they wear, or how they appear, this organ will be found small.

FIRMNESS can best be found by the following rule: Let the subject sit or stand erect, and hold the head in a line with the spinal column; then take the opening of the ear as your starting point, draw a line straight upward till you reach the middle line on the top of the head, and you are on the fore part of Firmness. When this organ is large, and Veneration is small, you will find its forward termination to resemble, in shape, the fore part of a smoothing-iron, rapidly widening as it runs backward; the organ is usually about an inch and a half long.

To find SELF-ESTEEM, take the junction of this perpendicular line with the middle line of the head, and an inch and a half backward will be found the upper part of Self-Esteem, which gives a lofty, aspiring air, magnanimity, and a determination to do something worthy of itself; while half an inch farther back will be found another part of Self-Esteem, which gives WILL, love of liberty, and a determination not to be ruled.

On the two sides of Self-Esteem, about an inch outwardly, APPROBATIVENESS is located. These two lobes run backward toward Adhesiveness, and upward toward Conscientiousness.

The relative size of Approbativeness and Self-Esteem may be found thus: Place one hand, say the left, upon the forehead, and steady the head; point the finger from above directly down upon Firmness; then move it two inches directly backward, and place the balls of the second and third fingers upon the points just found. If Self-Esteem be small, these balls will fall into the hole which indicates its deficiency, while the ends of the fingers will strike upon the swells caused by Approbativeness, if this organ be large; and the middle of the second joint of these fingers will apprehend the size of that lobe of Approbativeness which is next to it. Or thus: Stand behind the patient, and so place your fingers upon his head that the second finger shall reach upward to the back part of Firmness, then lay the first and second joints of that finger evenly with the head, and place the first and third fingers upon the head alongside of it. If Self-Esteem be larger than Approbativeness, the second finger will be pushed up farther than the others; but if the two lobes of Approbativeness be larger than Self-Esteem, the second finger will fall into a hollow running up and down, while the first and third fingers will rest upon the two lobes of Approbativeness. Or thus: In nineteen females out of every twenty, Self-Esteem will be found small and Approbativeness large, and by applying this rule to their heads, a hollow will generally be found at Self-Esteem and a swell at Approbativeness, by which you can localize these organs; and a few applications will soon enable you to form correct ideas of their appearance when large or small.

HOPE and CONSCIENTIOUSNESS are found thus: That line already drawn to find Firmness passes over the back part of Hope, which is on each side of the fore part of Firmness, while Conscientiousness is just back of that line, on the two sides of the back part of Firmness, joining Approbativeness behind.

As these two organs run lengthwise from Firmness down toward Cautiousness, and are near together, it is sometimes difficult to say which is large and which small. The upper part of Conscientiousness, next to Firmness, experiences feelings of obligation to God, or sense of duty to obey his laws; while the lower part creates a feeling of obligation to our fellow-men.

Near the middle of the top of the head is VENERATION, or about an inch forward of the point already described for finding Firmness; while BENEVOLENCE is about an inch forward of Veneration. When, therefore, the middle of the top head rounds out and rises above Firmness and Benevolence, Veneration is larger than either of these organs; but when there is a swell at Benevolence, and a depression as you pass backward in the middle of the head, and another rise as you pass still farther back to Firmness, Veneration is smaller than Benevolence or Firmness. The back of Benevolence experiences a desire to do good and to remove evil, while the fore part bestows minor gifts in the family and neighborhood. The fore part of Veneration gives respect for our fellow-men, while the back part supplicates and depends upon a Deity. The fore part of Firmness, working with Conscientiousness, gives moral decision; while the latter, acting with Self-Esteem, gives physical decision, determination to accomplish material objects, and what we commonly call perseverance.

On each side of Veneration, SPIRITUALITY is located. It may be found by the following rules: Standing behind the subject, who should be seated, so place your fingers that the first fingers of each hand shall be about an inch apart—that the ends of your second fingers shall be about three quarters of an inch forward of a line drawn across the middle of the head from side to side, and the balls of your fingers will be on Spirituality. Or reversing your position, so as to stand in FRONT of the subject, so place your hands that the first fingers of each hand shall be as before, about an inch apart, and the ends of your longest fingers shall just touch the fore part of Hope, and the balls of your second and third fingers will rest on Spirituality. This organ is generally small, so that it may usually be found by that depression which indicates its absence. When it is large, the head is filled out in this region, instead of sloping rapidly from Veneration. Its two lobes are about an inch on each side of Veneration, and directly above Ideality.

IMITATION is upon the two sides of Benevolence, directly forward of

Spirituality. The best rule for finding it is this: Standing in front of the subject, place your hands so that the first fingers of each hand shall be separated about three quarters of an inch, and that the end of your longest finger shall reach a line drawn through Veneration and Spirituality—that is, through the middle of the head from side to side—and the balls of your fingers will be on Imitation. It will be found large, or very large, in almost all children; so that the ridge usually found in their heads at this point, may be taken as the location of this organ. It runs from Benevolence downward toward Constructiveness. The upper part, toward Benevolence, mimics; the lower part, toward Constructiveness, is the the organ for making after a pattern, copying, etc.

We are now brought to the intellectual lobe. Take the root of the nose as your starting point; the first organ we meet in passing upward is INDIVIDUALITY. It is between the eyebrows, and when large, causes them to arch DOWNWARD at their inner termination.

Three quarters of an inch upward, and slightly below the centre of the forehead is EVENTUALITY, which in children is usually large, and in adults generally small. From this centre of the forehead, COMPARISON extends upward to where the head begins to slope backward to form the top of the head; at which point, or between Benevolence and Comparison, HUMAN NATURE is located, which is usually large in the American head, as is also Comparison. AGREEABLENESS, is located about an inch on each side of the organ of Human Nature, and is usually small; so that we can ascertain its location by observing its deficiency. When both of these organs are large, the forehead, will be wide and full as it rounds backward to form the top head, or where the hair makes its appearance. CAUSALITY is located about an inch on each side of Comparison; and MIRTHFULNESS about three quarters of an inch still farther outwardly toward Ideality. FORM is located internally from Individuality, just above and partly between the eyes, so as to set them wider apart, in proportion as it is larger or smaller.

SIZE is located just in the turn between the nose and eyebrows, or beneath the inner portion of the eyebrows; and when large, causes their inner portions to project outward over the inner portion of the eyes like the eaves of a house, giving to the eyes a sunken appearance. Size can generally be observed by sight, yet if you would test your sight by touch, proceed as follows: Place the end of your thumb against the bridge of your nose, with the lower part of your hand turned outward, and your thumb lying nearly parallel with the eyebrows, and the balls of your thumb will be upon Size. And if this organ be large, you will observe a fullness in this region, as if half a bean were beneath your thumb.

To find WEIGHT and COLOR, proceed as follows: Let the eyes be directed straight forward, as if looking at some object; draw an imaginary line from the middle of the eye to the eyebrow; internally from this line beneath the eyebrows Weight is located, while Color is located beneath the eyebrows just outwardly from this line. ORDER is located just externally to Color: and TIME is located partly above and between Color and Order This organ is small in most heads.

CALCULATION is located beneath the outer termination of the eyebrows, and in proportion as they are long and extend backward to the eye, will this organ be more or less developed. Three fourths of an inch ABOVE the outer angle of the eyebrow, TUNE is located. Spurzheim's rule for finding it is this: Stand directly before the subject, and if the head widens over the outer eyebrow as you rise upward, Tune is large; but if you observe a hollow at this point, Tune is small. I have generally found this organ small in adults, so that it is difficult to find its relative size, but in children it is very easily found; its decline is consequent on its non-exercise. Time and Tune join each other, while Time, Tune, and Mirthfulness occupy the three angles of a triangle, nearly equilateral, the shortest side being between Time and Tune.

LANGUAGE is located partly above and partly behind the eyes. When it is large, it pushes the eyes downward and outward, and of course shoves them forward, which gives them a full and swollen appearance, as if they were standing partly out of their sockets, and causes both the upper and under eyelids to be wide and broad. When the eyes are sunken, and their lids narrow, Language will be found small.

By following these rules exactly and specifically, the precise location of the organs can be ascertained, and a few observations upon heads will soon teach you the appearance of the respective organs when they are large, small, or midway in size. Some slight allowances are to be made, however, in calculating the size of the head, or the relative size of the organs. Thus, the larger Combativeness is, the longer the line from Combativeness to the ear; yet large and small Combativeness do not vary this line over from a quarter to half an inch; so that there will be but little difficulty in finding the precise location of this organ.

Probably the most difficult point of discrimination is between Hope and Conscientiousness, and it should be distinctly borne in mind, that Hope is generally placed too far forward. Between Hope, Cautiousness, and Approbativeness, there probably exists an organ, the natural functions of which has not yet been fully established. There are doubtless other organs yet undiscovered, especially in the middle line of the head, between Benevolence and Philoprogenitiveness, and also between Imitation and Causality. Phrenology is yet in its infancy. Though it is perfect in itself, yet our KNOWLEDGE of it is not yet perfected. As every successive generation make advances upon one another in Astronomy, Chemistry, and other departments of science, so Gall and Spurzheim have discovered only the landmarks of this science and have left much to be filled up by us, and those who come after us.

BOSTON: 142 Washington St.

PHILADELPHIA: 231 Arch Street.

IN order to accommodate "The People" residing in all parts of the United States, the Publishers will forward by return of the FIRST MAIL, any book named in this List. The postage will be prepaid by them at the New York Post-Office. By this arrangement of paying postage in advance, fifty per cent. is saved to the purchaser. The price of each work, including postage, is given, so that the exact amount may be remitted. Fractional parts of a dollar may be sent in postage-stamps. All letters containing orders should be post-paid, and directed as follows: **FOWLERS AND WELLS, 308 Broadway, New York.**

WORKS ON PHRENOLOGY.

AMERICAN PHRENOLOGICAL JOURNAL. A REPOSITORY OF Science, Literature, and General Intelligence; Devoted to Phrenology, Physiology, Education, Mechanism, Agriculture, and to all those Progressive Measures which are calculated to Reform, Elevate, and Improve Mankind. Illustrated with Numerous Engravings. Quarto, suitable for binding. 288 pp. Published Monthly, at One Dollar a Year.

It may be termed the standard authority in all matters pertaining to Phrenology, while the beautiful typography of the Journal, and the superior character of the numerous illustrations, are not exceeded in any work with which we are acquainted.—*American Courier, Phila.*

COMBE'S LECTURE ON PHRENOLOGY. BY GEORGE COMBE. WITH Notes, an Essay on the Phrenological Mode of Investigation, and an Historical Sketch. By Andrew Boardman, M.D. 12mo., 391 pp. Illustrated. Muslin, $1 25.

CHART, FOR RECORDING THE VARIOUS PHRENOLOGICAL DEVELopments. Illustrated with Engravings. Designed for the use of Phrenologists. Price, 6 cts.

CONSTITUTION OF MAN, CONSIDERED IN RELATION TO EXTERNAL Objects. By George Combe. The only authorized American Edition. With Twenty Engravings, and a Portrait of the Author. Paper, 62 cents; Muslin, 87 cents.

THREE HUNDRED THOUSAND COPIES of this great work have been sold, and the demand still increases.

CONSTITUTION OF MAN. BY GEORGE COMBE. ABRIDGED AND Adapted to the Use of Schools, with Questions. To which is added an Appendix descriptive of the Five Principal Races of Men. School Edition, in boards. Price, 30 cents.

The "Constitution of Man" is a work with which every teacher and every pupil should be acquainted. It contains a perfect mine of sound wisdom and enlightened philosophy; and a faithful study of its invaluable lessons would save many a promising youth from a premature grave.—*Journal of Education, Albany, N. Y.*

DEFENCE OF PHRENOLOGY. CONTAINING AN ESSAY ON THE Nature and Value of Phrenological Evidence; also, an able Vindication of Phrenology. By Andrew Boardman. Muslin, 87 cents.

DOMESTIC LIFE. THOUGHTS ON ITS CONCORD AND DISCORD, with Valuable Hints and Suggestions. By N. Sizer. Price, 15 cents.

EDUCATION COMPLETE. EMBRACING PHYSIOLOGY, ANIMAL AND Mental, applied to the Preservation and Restoration of Health of Body and Power of Mind; Self-Culture, and Perfection of Character, including the Management of Youth; Memory and Intellectual Improvement, applied to Self-Education and Juvenile Instruction. By O. S. Fowler. Complete in one large volume. Muslin, $2 50.

Every one should read it who would preserve or restore his health, develop his mind, and improve his character.

EDUCATION: ITS ELEMENTARY PRINCIPLES FOUNDED ON THE Nature of Man. By J. G. Spurzheim, M. D. With an Appendix, containing a Description of the Temperaments, and an Analysis of the Phrenological Faculties. Muslin, 87 cents.

We regard this volume as one of the most important that has been offered to the public for many years. It is full of sound doctrines and practical wisdom.—*Boston Med. and Sur. Jour.*

FAMILIAR LESSONS ON PHRENOLOGY AND PHYSIOLOGY; FOR Children and Youth. Two volumes in one. By Mrs. L. N. Fowler. Muslin, $1 25.

The natural language of each organ is illustrated with wood-cuts, and the work is brought out in a style well adapted to the family circle, as well as the school-room.—*Teachers' Companion.*

LOVE AND PARENTAGE; APPLIED TO THE IMPROVEMENT OF Offspring: including important Directions to Lovers and the Married, concerning the strongest Ties, and most sacred and momentous Relations of Life. By O. S. Fowler. Price, 30 cts.

LOVE, PARENTAGE, AND AMATIVENESS. ONE VOL. MUSLIN, 75 CENTS.

MENTAL SCIENCE. LECTURES ON THE PHILOSOPHY OF PHRENOLOGY. By Rev. G. S. Weaver. Illustrated with Engravings. Muslin, 87 cents.

These Lectures were prepared for the intellectual, moral, and social benefit of society. The author has, in this respect, done a good work for the rising generation.

MORAL AND INTELLECTUAL SCIENCE; APPLIED TO THE ELEVATION of Society. By George Combe, Robert Cox, and others. Large octavo. Price, $2 30.

This work contains Essays on Phrenology, as a department of physiological science, exhibiting its varied and important applications to interesting questions of social and moral philosophy, to legislation, medicine, and the arts. With Portraits of Drs. Gall, Spurzheim, and Combe.

MARRIAGE: ITS HISTORY AND PHILOSOPHY. WITH A PHRENOlogical and Physiological Exposition of the Functions and Qualifications necessary for Happy Marriages. By L. N. Fowler. Illustrated. Muslin. Price, 75 cents.

It contains a full account of the marriage forms and ceremonies of all nations and tribes, from the earliest history down to the present time. Those who have not yet entered into matrimonial relations should read this book, and all may profit by a perusal.—*N. Y. Illustrated Magazine.*

MEMORY AND INTELLECTUAL IMPROVEMENT; APPLIED TO SELF-Education and Juvenile Instruction. By O. S. Fowler. Twentieth Edition. Enlarged and Improved. Illustrated with Engravings. Price, 87 cents.

The science of Phrenology, now so well established, affords us important aid in developing the human mind, according to the natural laws of our being. This, the work before us is pre-eminently calculated to promote, and we cordially recommend it to all.—*Democratic Review.*

MATRIMONY; OR, PHRENOLOGY AND PHYSIOLOGY APPLIED TO the Selection of Congenial Companions for Life; including Directions to the Married for Living together Affectionately and Happily. By O. S. Fowler. Price, 30 cents.

Upwards of sixty thousand copies having been sold in the United States, besides having been republished in London, no man or woman, married or unmarried, should fail to possess a copy.

PHRENOLOGY PROVED, ILLUSTRATED, AND APPLIED; ACCOMPAnied by a Chart, embracing an Analysis of the Primary Mental Powers in their Various Degrees of Development, the Phenomena produced by their Combined Activity, and the Location of the Phrenological Organs in the Head. Together with a View of the Moral and Theological Bearing of the Science. By O. S. and L. N. Fowler. Price, $1 25.

This is a PRACTICAL, STANDARD Work, and may be described as a complete system of the principles and practice of Phrenology. Besides important remarks on the Temperaments, it contains a description of all the primary mental powers, in seven different degrees of development, together with the combinations of the faculties; in short, we regard this work as not only the most important of any which has before been written on the science, but as indispensably necessary to the student who wishes to acquire a thorough knowledge of Phrenological Science.

PHRENOLOGICAL ALMANAC. PUBLISHED ANNUALLY. WITH CALendars for all Latitudes. Profusely Illustrated with Portraits of Distinguished Persons. 6 cts.

POPULAR PHRENOLOGY; EXHIBITING THE PHRENOLOGICAL ADmeasurements of above Fifty Distinguished and Extraordinary Personages of Both Sexes. With numerous Portraits and other Illustrations. By Frederick Coombs. Price, 30 cents.

PHRENOLOGICAL BUST; DESIGNED ESPECIALLY FOR LEARNERS. Showing the Exact Location of all the Organs of the Brain fully developed. Price, including box for packing, $1 25. [May be sent by Express. Not mailable.]

This is one of the most ingenious inventions of the age. A cast made of plaster of Paris, the size of the human head, on which the exact location of each of the Phrenological organs is represented, fully developed, with all the divisions and classifications. Those who cannot obtain the services of a professor may learn in a very short time, from this model head, the science of Phrenology, so far as the location of the organs is concerned.—*N. Y. Sun.*

PHRENOLOGY AND THE SCRIPTURES; SHOWING THEIR HARMONY. An able, though small work. By Rev. John Pierpont. Price, 12 cents.

PHRENOLOGICAL GUIDE. DESIGNED FOR STUDENTS OF THEIR own Characters. With numerous illustrative Engravings. Price, 15 cents.

PHRENOLOGY AND PHYSIOLOGY; A SYNOPSIS, COMPRISING A CONdensed Description of the Functions of the Body and Mind. By L. N. Fowler. Price, 15 cts.

PHRENOLOGICAL SPECIMENS FOR PHRENOLOGICAL SOCIETIES AND Private Cabinets. We have made a selection of forty of our best specimens, among which are casts from the head, size of life, of John Quincy Adams, Aaron Burr, George Combe, Elihu Burritt, T. H. Benton, Henry Clay, Rev. Dr. Dodd, Thomas A. Emmett, Dr. Gall, Sylvester Graham, J. C. Neal, Walter Scott, Voltaire, Silas Wright, Black Hawk, etc., etc. Phrenological Societies can expend a small sum in no better way than by procuring this set, as they have been selected particularly with reference to showing the contrasts of the Phrenological developments in different characters. They can be packed, and sent as freight or by express, with perfect safety, to any place desired. Price, only $25 00.

RELIGION, NATURAL AND REVEALED; OR, THE NATURAL THEO-logy and Moral Bearings of Phrenology, including the Doctrines taught and Duties inculcated thereby, compared with those enjoined in the Scriptures: with an Exposition of the Doctrines of a Future State, Materialism, Holiness, Sins, Rewards, Punishments, Depravity, a Change of Heart, Will, Foreordination, and Fatalism. By O. S. Fowler. Price, 87 cents.

If ever our various religious opinions are to be brought into harmonious action, it must be done through the instrumentality of Phrenological Science.—*Christian Freeman.*

SELF-CULTURE, AND PERFECTION OF CHARACTER; INCLUDING the Education and Management of Youth. By O. S. Fowler. Price, 87 cents.

"SELF-MADE, OR NEVER MADE," is the motto No individual can read a page of it without being improved thereby. With this work, in connection with PHYSIOLOGY, ANIMAL AND MENTAL, AND MEMORY, AND INTELLECTUAL IMPROVEMENT, we may become fully acquainted with ourselves, comprehending, as they do, the whole man. We advise all to read these works.—*Com. School Adv.*

SELF-INSTRUCTOR IN PHRENOLOGY AND PHYSIOLOGY. ILLUS-trated with One Hundred Engravings; including a Chart for recording the various Degrees of Development. By O. S. and L. N. Fowler. Price in Paper, 30 cents; Muslin, 50 cents.

This treatise is emphatically a book for the million. It contains an explanation of each faculty, full enough to be clear, yet so short as not to weary; together with combinations of the faculties, and engravings to show the organs, large and small; thereby enabling all persons, with little study, to become acquainted with practical Phrenology. An excellent work for students.

SYMBOLICAL HEAD AND PHRENOLOGICAL CHART, IN MAP FORM. Showing the Natural Language of the Phrenological Organs. Price, 25 cents.

TEMPERANCE AND TIGHT LACING: FOUNDED ON PHRENOLOGY and Physiology, showing the Injurious Effects of Stimulants, and the Evils inflicted on the Human Constitution by compressing the Organs of Animal Life. With Numerous Illustrations. By O. S. Fowler. Price, 15 cents.

Should be placed in the pews of every church in the land. The two curses, intemperance and bad fashions, are destroying more human beings yearly, than all other causes; to arrest which, these little (great) works will render effectual aid.—*Dr. Beecher.*

THE WORKS OF GALL, COMBE, SPURZHEIM, AND OTHERS, WITH all the works on Phrenology, for sale, wholesale and retail. 308 Broadway, New York.

FOWLERS AND WELLS have all works on PHRENOLOGY, PHYSIOLOGY, HYDROPATHY, and the Natural Sciences generally. Booksellers supplied on the most liberal terms. AGENTS wanted in every State, county, and town. These works are universally popular, and thousands might be sold where they have never yet been introduced.

Letters and other communications should, in ALL CASES, be post-paid, and directed to the Publishers, as follows: **FOWLER, AND WELLS, 308 Broadway, New York.**

CHOLERA: ITS CAUSES, PREVENTION, AND CURE; SHOWING THE Inefficiency of Drug-Treatment, and the Superiority of the Water-Cure in this and in all other Bowel Diseases. By Dr. Shew. Price, 30 cents.

DOMESTIC PRACTICE OF HYDROPATHY, WITH FIFTEEN ENGRAVED Illustrations of Important Subjects, with a Form of a Report for the Assistance of Patients in consulting their Physicians by Correspondence. By Ed. Johnson, M. D. Muslin, $1 50.

EXPERIENCE IN WATER-CURE; A FAMILIAR EXPOSITION OF THE Principles and Results of Water-Treatment in Acute and Chronic Diseases; an Explanation of Water-Cure Processes; Advice on Diet and Regimen, and Particular Directions to Women in the Treatment of Female Diseases, Water-Treatment in Childbirth, and the Diseases of Infancy. Illustrated by Numerous Cases. By Mrs. Nichols. Price, 30 cents.

ERRORS OF PHYSICIANS AND OTHERS IN THE PRACTICE OF THE Water-Cure. By J. H. Rausse. Translated from the German. Price, 30 cents.

HYDROPATHIC FAMILY PHYSICIAN. A READY PRESCRIBER AND Hygienic Adviser, with reference to the Nature, Causes, Prevention and Treatment of Diseases, Accidents, and Casualties of every kind; with a Glossary, Table of Contents, and Index. Illustrated with nearly Three Hundred Engravings. By Joel Shew, M.D. One large volume of 820 pages, substantially bound, in library style. Price, with postage prepaid by mail, $2 50.

It possesses the most practical utility of any of the author's contributions to popular medicine. and is well adapted to give the reader an accurate idea of the organization and functions of the human frame.—*New York Tribune.*

HYDROPATHY FOR THE PEOPLE. WITH PLAIN OBSERVATIONS ON Drugs, Diet, Water, Air, and Exercise. A popular Work, by Wm. Horsell, of London. With Notes and Observations by Dr. Trall. Muslin, 87 cents.

HYDROPATHY: OR, THE WATER-CURE. ITS PRINCIPLES, PRO-cesses and Modes of Treatment. In part from the most Eminent Authors, Ancient and Modern. Together with an Account of the Latest Methods of Priessnitz. Numerous Cases, with full Treatment described. By Dr. Shew. 12mo. Muslin, $1 25.

HOME TREATMENT FOR SEXUAL ABUSES. A PRACTICAL TREA-tise for both Sexes, on the Nature and Causes of Excessive and Unnatural Indulgence, the Diseases and Injuries resulting therefrom, with their Symptoms and Hydropathic Management. By Dr. Trall. Price, 30 cents.

HYDROPATHIC ENCYCLOPÆDIA: A SYSTEM OF HYDROPATHY AND Hygiene. Containing Outlines of Anatomy; Physiology of the Human Body; Hygienic Agencies, and the Preservation of Health; Dietetics, and Hydropathic Cookery; Theory and Practice of Water-Treatment; Special Pathology, and Hydro-Therapeutics, including the Nature, Causes, Symptoms, and Treatment of all known Diseases; Application of Hydropathy to Midwifery and the Nursery. Designed as a Guide to Families and Students, and a Text-Book for Physicians. By R. T. Trall, M. D. Illustrated with upwards of Three Hundred Engravings and Colored Plates. Substantially bound, in one large volume, also in two 12mo. vols. Price for either edition, prepaid by mail, in Muslin, $3 00; in Leather, $3 50.

This is the most comprehensive and popular work yet published on the subject of Hydropathy, with nearly one thousand pages. Of all the numerous publications which have attained such a wide popularity, as issued by Fowlers and Wells, perhaps none are more adapted to general utility than this rich, comprehensive, and well-arranged Encyclopædia.—*N. Y. Tribune.*

HYDROPATHIC QUARTERLY REVIEW. A PROFESSIONAL MAGAZINE, devoted to Medical Reform; embracing Articles by the best Writers on Anatomy, Physiology, Pathology, Surgery, Therapeutics, Midwifery, etc.; Reports of Remarkable Cases in General Practice, Criticisms on the Theory and Practice of the various Opposing Systems of Medical Science, Reviews of New Publications of all Schools of Medicine, Reports of the Progress of Health Reform in all its aspects, etc., with appropriate Engraved Illustrations. Terms, a Year, in advance, Two Dollars.

Filled with articles of permanent value which ought to be read by every American.—*N. Y. Trib.*

HYGIENE AND HYDROPATHY. THREE LECTURES. FULL OF Interest and Instruction. By R. S. Houghton, M. D. Price, 30 cents.

INTRODUCTION TO THE WATER-CURE. FOUNDED IN NATURE, AND adapted to the Wants of Man. By Dr. Nichols. Price, 15 cents.

MIDWIFERY, AND THE DISEASES OF WOMEN. A DESCRIPTIVE AND Practical Work, showing the Superiority of Water-Treatment in Menstruation and its Disorders, Chlorosis, Leucorrhœa, Fluor Albus, Prolapsis Uteri, Hysteria, Spinal Diseases and other Weaknesses of Females; in Pregnancy and its Diseases, Abortion, Uterine Hemorrhage, and the General Management of Childbirth, Nursing, etc., etc. Illustrated with Numerous Cases of Treatment. By Joel Shew, M. D. 12mo. 432 pp. Muslin, $1 25.

PARENTS' GUIDE FOR THE TRANSMISSION OF DESIRED QUALITIES to Offspring, and Childbirth made Easy. By Mrs. Hester Pendleton. Price, 60 cents.

PRACTICE OF WATER-CURE. WITH AUTHENTICATED EVIDENCE of its Efficacy and Safety. Containing a detailed account of the various processes used in the Water-Treatment, etc. By James Wilson, M. D., and James M. Gully, M. D. 30 cents.

PHILOSOPHY OF WATER CURE. A DEVELOPMENT OF THE TRUE Principles of Health and Longevity. By John Balbirnie, M. D. With a Letter from Sir Edward Lytton Bulwer. From the Second London Edition. Paper. Price, 30 cents.

PREGNANCY AND CHILDBIRTH. ILLUSTRATED WITH CASES, SHOWing the Remarkable Effects of Water in Mitigating the Pains and Perils of the Parturient State. By Dr. Shew. Paper. Price, 30 cents.

PRINCIPLES OF HYDROPATHY: OR, THE INVALID'S GUIDE TO Health and Happ ess. Being a plain, familiar Exposition of the Principles of the Water-Cure System. By David A. Harsha. Price, 15 cents.

RESULTS OF HYDROPATHY; OR, CONSTIPATION NOT A DISEASE of the Bowel , Indigestion not a Disease of the Stomach; with an Exposition of the true Nature and C uses of these Ailments, explaining the reason why they are so certainly cured by the Hydr pathic Treatment. By Edward Johnson, M. D. Muslin. Price, 87 cents.

SCIENCE OF SWIMMING. GIVING A HISTORY OF SWIMMING, AND Instructions to Learners. By an Experienced Swimmer. Illustrated with Engravings. 15 cts.

Every boy in the nation should have a copy, and learn to swim.

WATER-CURE LIBRARY. (IN SEVEN 12MO. VOLUMES.) EMBRACING the most popular works on the subject. By American and European Authors. Bound in Embossed Muslin, Library Style. Price, prepaid by mail, only $7 00.

This library comprises most of the important works on the subject of Hydropathy. The volumes are of uniform size and binding, and the whole form a most valuable medical library.

WATER-CURE IN AMERICA. OVER THREE HUNDRED CASES OF various Diseases treated with Water by Drs. Wesselhœft, Shew, Bedortha, Trall, and others. With Cases of Domestic Practice. Designed for Popular as well as Professional Reading. Edited by a Water Patient. Muslin, $1 25.

WATER AND VEGETABLE DIET IN CONSUMPTION, SCROFULA, Cancer, Asthma, and other Chronic Diseases. In which the Advantages of Pure Water are particularly considered. By William Lambe, M. D. With Notes and Additions by Joel Shew, M. D. 12mo. 258 pp. Paper, 62 cents; Muslin, 87 cents.

WATER-CURE APPLIED TO EVERY KNOWN DISEASE. A NEW Theory. A Complete Demonstration of the Advantages of the Hydropathic System of Curing Diseases; showing also the fallacy of the Allopathic Method, and its Utter Inability to Effect a Permanent Cure. With Appendix, containing Hydropathic Diet, and Rules for Bathing. By J. H. Rausse. Translated from the German. Muslin, 87 cents.

WATER-CURE MANUAL. A POPULAR WORK, EMBRACING Descriptions of the Various Modes of Bathing, the Hygienic and Curative Effects of Air, Exercise, Clothing, Occupation, Diet, Water-Drinking, etc. Together with Descriptions of Diseases, and the Hydropathic Remedies. By Joel Shew, M. D. Muslin. Price, 87 cents.

WATER-CURE ALMANAC. PUBLISHED ANNUALLY, CONTAINING Important and Valuable Hydropathic Matter. Illustrated with Numerous Engravings, with correct calculations for all latitudes. 48 pp. Price, 6 cents.

WATER-CURE JOURNAL, AND HERALD OF REFORMS. DEVOTED TO Physiology, Hydropathy, and the Laws of Life and Health. Illustrated with Numerous Engravings. Quarto. Published Monthly, at $1 00 a Year, in advance.

We know of no American periodical which presents a greater abundance of valuable information on all subjects relating to human progress and welfare.—*N. Y. Tribune.*

This is, unquestionably, the most popular Health Journal in the world.—*N. Y. Evening Post.*

FOWLERS AND WELLS have all works on PHYSIOLOGY, HYDROPATHY, PHRENOLOGY, and the Natural Sciences generally. Booksellers supplied on the most liberal terms. AGENTS wanted in every State, county, and town. These works are universally popular, and thousands might be sold where they have never yet been introduced.

Letters and other communications should, in ALL CASES, be post-paid, and directed to the Publishers, as follows:

FOWLER AND WELLS, 308 Broadway, New York.

NATURAL HISTORY OF MAN. SHOWING HIS THREE ASPECTS OF Plant, Beast, and Angel. Plant Life, comprising the Nutritive Apparatus. Beast Life, or Soul, the Phrenological Faculties. Angel Life, or Spirit, Jehovah's likeness in Man. By John B. Newman, M. D. Illustrated with Engravings. Price, 87 cents.

PHYSIOLOGY, ANIMAL AND MENTAL. APPLIED TO THE PRESERVAtion and Restoration of Health of Body and Power of Mind. By O. S. Fowler. Illustrated with Engravings. Price 87 cents.

REPRODUCTIVE ORGANS. THEIR DISEASES, CAUSES, AND CURE on Hydropathic Principles. By James C. Jackson. Price 15 cents.

SEXUAL DISEASES; THEIR CAUSES, PREVENTION AND CURE, ON Physiological Principles. Embracing Home Treatment for Sexual Abuses; Chronic Diseases, Especially the Nervous Diseases of Women; The Philosophy of Generation; Amativeness; Hints on the Reproductive Organs. In one volume. Price, $1 25 cents.

SOBER AND TEMPERATE LIFE. THE DISCOURSES AND LETTERS OF Louis Cornaro. With a Biography of the Author. With Notes, and an Appendix. 30 cts. Twenty-five thousand copies have been sold. It is translated into several languages.

TOBACCO: ITS HISTORY, NATURE, AND EFFECTS ON THE BODY and Mind. With the Opinions of the Rev. Dr. Nott, L. N. Fowler, Rev. Henry Ward Beecher, Horace Greeley, Dr. Jennings, O. S. Fowler, Dr. R. T. Trall, and others. By Joel Shew, M. D. Price, 30 cents.

TOBACCO. THREE PRIZE ESSAYS. BY DRS. SHEW, TRALL, AND Rev. D. Baldwin. Price, 15 cents. Per hundred, $3 00.

TEMPERANCE TRACTS. BY TRALL, GREELEY, BARNUM, FOWLER, and others. Price, per hundred, 75 cents. Per thousand, by Express, $4 00.

TEETH: THEIR STRUCTURE, DISEASE, AND TREATMENT. WITH numerous Illustrations. By John Burdell. Price 15 cents.

TEA AND COFFEE. THEIR PHYSICAL, INTELLECTUAL, AND MORAL Effects on the Human System. By Dr. William A. Alcott. Price, 15 cents.

USE OF TOBACCO; ITS PHYSICAL, INTELLECTUAL, AND MORAL Effects on the Human System. By Dr. William A. Alcott. Price, 15 cents.

VEGETABLE DIET; AS SANCTIONED BY MEDICAL MEN, AND BY Experience in all Ages. Including a System of Vegetable Cookery. By Dr. Alcott. 87 cts.

UTERINE DISEASES: OR, THE DISPLACEMENT OF THE UTERUS. A thorough and practical treatise on the Malpositions of the Uterus and adjacent Organs. Illustrated with Colored Engravings from Original Designs. By R. T. Trall. M. D. Price, $5 00.

EITHER OF THESE WORKS may be ordered and received by return of the FIRST MAIL, postage prepaid by the Publishers, FOWLER AND WELLS, 308 Broadway, New York.

MESMERISM AND PSYCHOLOGY.

A NEW AND COMPLETE LIBRARY OF MESMERISM AND PSYchology, embracing the most popular works on the subject, with suitable Illustrations. In two volumes of about 900 pp. Bound in Library Style. Price, $3 00.

BIOLOGY; OR, THE PRINCIPLES OF THE HUMAN MIND. DEDUCED from Physical Laws, and on the Voltaic Mechanism of Man. Illustrated. Price, 30 cents.

ELECTRICAL PSYCHOLOGY, PHILOSOPHY OF. IN A COURSE OF Twelve Lectures. By John Bovee Dods. Muslin. Price, 87 cents.

FASCINATION; OR, THE PHILOSOPHY OF CHARMING. ILLUSTRATing the Principles of Life, in connection with Spirit and Matter. By J. B. Newman, M.D. 87 cts.

MENTAL ALCHEMY. A TREATISE ON THE MIND, NERVOUS SYSTEM, Psychology, Magnetism, Mesmerism, and Diseases. By B. B. Williams, M.D. Price, 62 cts.

MACROCOSM AND MICROCOSM; OR, THE UNIVERSE WITHOUT AND the Universe Within: in the World of Sense, and the World of Soul. By Wm. Fishbough. Price, Paper, 62 cents. Muslin, 87 cents.

PHILOSOPHY OF MESMERISM. SIX LECTURES. WITH AN INTROduction. By Rev. John Bovee Dods. Paper. Price, 30 cents.

PSYCHOLOGY; OR, THE SCIENCE OF THE SOUL. CONSIDERED Physiologically and Philosophically. With an Appendix containing Notes of Mesmeric and Psychical Experience. By Joseph Haddock, M. D. With Engravings. Price, 30 cents

SPIRITUAL INTERCOURSE, PHILOSOPHY OF. BEING AN EXPLANAtion of Modern Mysteries. By Andrew Jackson Davis. Price, 62 cents.

SUPERNAL THEOLOGY, AND LIFE IN THE SPHERES. DEDUCED from alleged Spiritual Manifestations. By Owen G. Warren. Octavo. Price 30 cents.

MISCELLANEOUS.

BOTANY FOR ALL CLASSES. CONTAINING A FLORAL DICTIONARY, and a Glossary of Scientific Terms. Illustrated. By J. B. Newman, M.D. Price, 87 cents.

CHEMISTRY, AND ITS APPLICATIONS TO AGRICULTURE AND Commerce. By Justus Liebig, M. D., F. R. S. Price, 25 cents.

DELIA'S DOCTORS; OR, A GLANCE BEHIND THE SCENES. BY Hannah Gardner Creamer. Paper. Price, 62 cents. Muslin, 87 cents.

FAMILIAR LESSONS ON ASTRONOMY: DESIGNED FOR THE USE of Children and Youth in Schools and Families. By Mrs. L. N. Fowler. Illustrated. 87 cts.

FUTURE OF NATIONS: IN WHAT CONSISTS ITS SECURITY. A Lecture delivered in the Tabernacle, New York. By Kossuth. With a Likeness. Price, 12 cts. WHAT THE SISTER ARTS TEACH AS TO FARMING. AN ADDRESS. By Horace Greeley. Price, 12 cents. TRUE BASIS OF AMERICAN INDEPENDENCE. AN ADDRESS. By Hon. Wm. H. Seward. Price, 12 cents. ESSAY ON WAGES. The Means Employed for Upholding Them. By P. C. Friese. Price, 15 cts. LABOR, ITS HISTORY AND PROSPECTS. By Robert Dale Owen. Price, 30 cents.

HINTS TOWARDS REFORMS; CONSISTING OF LECTURES, ESsays, Addresses, and other Writings. With the Crystal Palace, and its Lessons. Second Edition, Enlarged. ByHorace Greeley. Price, $1 25.

HOPES AND HELPS FOR THE YOUNG OF BOTH SEXES. RELATING to the Formation of Character, Choice of Avocation, Health, Amusement, Music, Conversation, Cultivation of Intellect, Moral Sentiments, Social Affection, Courtship and Marriage. By Rev. G. S. Weaver. Price, in Paper, 62 cents. Muslin, 87 cents.

HUMAN RIGHTS, AND THEIR POLITICAL GUARANTIES. BY Judge Hurlbut. With Notes, by George Combe. Price, Paper, 62 cents. Muslin, 87 cts.

HOME FOR ALL. A NEW, CHEAP, CONVENIENT, AND SUPERIOR Mode of Building, containing full Directions for Constructing Gravel Walls. With Views, Plans, and Engraved Illustrations. New Edition, Revised and Enlarged. Price, 87 cents.

IMMORTALITY TRIUMPHANT. THE EXISTENCE OF A GOD AND Human Immortality, Practically Considered, and the Truth of Divine Revelation Substantiated. By Rev. John Bovee Dods. Price, Paper, 62 cents. Muslin, 87 cents.

LITERATURE AND ART. BY S. MARGARET FULLER. TWO PARTS in one volume. With an Introduction, by Horace Greeley. Muslin. Price, $1 25.

PHONOGRAPHIC TEACHER. PRICE, 45 CENTS. REPORTERS' MANual. 75 cents. And all other Works on Phonography. Wholesale and Retail.

POWER OF KINDNESS; INCULCATING THE PRINCIPLES OF Benevolence and Love. By Charles Morley. Paper, 30 cents. Muslin, 50 cents.

POPULATION, THEORY OF. DEDUCED FROM THE GENERAL LAW of Animal Fertility. With an Introduction by R. T. Trall, M. D. Price, 15 cents.

WOMAN; HER EDUCATION AND INFLUENCE. BY MRS. HUGO Reid. With an Introduction by Mrs. C. M. Kirkland. With Portraits. Price, 87 cents.

THESE works may be ordered in large or small quantities. A liberal discount will be made to AGENTS, and others, who buy to sell again. They may be sent by Express, or as Freight, by Railroad, Steamships, Sailing Vessels, by Stage or Canal, to any City, Town, or Village, in the United States, the Canadas, to Europe, or any place on the Globe.

Checks or drafts, for large amounts, on New York, Philadelphia, or Boston, always preferred. We pay cost of exchange. All letters should be post-paid, and addressed as follows;

FOWLER AND WELLS, 308 Broadway, New York.

www.ingramcontent.com/pod-product-compliance
Lightning Source LLC
LaVergne TN
LVHW021412110826
845150LV00007B/1893

* 9 7 8 1 4 2 5 5 1 1 4 8 7 *